W9-BTS-648

Contents

Chapter 1

Discovering the "Other Bulbs"

I WAS ABOUT TEN, I SUPPOSE, WHEN I GREW MY FIRST BULB. Miss Sharpley's fifth-grade class at Runnymede Public School had a project that year: to observe the fundamentals of botany by forcing bulbs in a dish of aquarium gravel and water. I dutifully begged my parents for fifty cents to buy a half dozen paperwhite bulbs. I remember bringing to school a glass cereal bowl into which I crammed the bulbs and filled around them with gravel.

The bowls, each labeled with a student's name, were lined up on a shelf at the back of the class with the arrowheads, stuffed owl, giant pine cones, and petrified wood samples that constituted our introduction to nature studies. At first, the bowls were covered to keep out the light, and it probably took more than a ten-year-old's discipline to remember to water them. But I recall that my fascination grew as my bowl filled with roots that began pushing the gravel up the sides of the container. When the bowls were uncovered and placed by the high, bright windows at the side of the classroom, green stems shot up dramatically.

Soon, the stems were joined by fat buds that one morning opened into starry white flowers. How proud and omnipotent I felt when those flowers glowed in the late-winter sun. Although I doubt that it was her intention, Miss Sharpley imparted an important lesson: by planting bulbs, I could bloom beautiful flowers with little effort and receive the accolades of many, as well as a healthy dollop of personal satisfaction. Her lesson would mark me for life as a bulb grower.

(Opposite page 1):
Hippeastrum hybrids. One of the
color forms of amaryllis.

Clivia miniata.

I started out with the old familiar bulbs. They were the same varieties my father was forced to dig the garden for in the autumn so that Mom could put in a few types that would herald the spring. I particularly remember garishly clashing tulips that came from a mixed packet. As my tastes matured, I planted snowdrops under the trees and clumps of hyacinths beside the front steps where they could be nosed without venturing too far out on our cool spring days. Daffodils and iris had their time, and, of course, paperwhites. But I've always been one of those gardeners who likes to try new things. That's how I discovered the "Other Bulbs" section of the catalog.

The Other Bulbs came to my attention when I received my first catalog from Mr. Cruickshank. Mr. Cruickshank was a helpful old local gentleman who owned the best-known bulb store in Canada at the time. This was not saying much, because the store occupied, as it still does, a modest front in one of the more genteel neighborhoods in Toronto. Mr. Cruickshank issued lovingly annotated bulb lists from this happy place. A good plant seller must also be a good writer because he must evoke in a few sentences an insatiable desire to have that plant. Mr. Cruickshank was very good, and I soon wanted to own almost every bulb he described.

I began to buy bulbs with names like *Clivia* (as in Clive of India) *miniata*, with its orange-red trumpets nestled in a bed of thick, dark green strapshaped leaves. It bloomed for more than a month in a pot occupying a shady corner of my deck. Once I'd mastered clivia, I had to have more. I tried *Eucharis grandiflora* (more like an Amazon daffodil than Amazon lily, which is one of its common names) and discovered that some bulbs needed hot, moist conditions to thrive. Then came eucomis, or pineapple lily, often sold as a summer patio plant. Now I grow not one, but three eucomis species, that bloom at different times in the summer and give me an almost continuous show, with flowers that vary from pink to burgundy-striped whites. As I bloomed each one of the Other Bulbs, the exotic pleasure of unusual flowers in the summer garden took hold.

I had unwittingly discovered a whole new world of bulbs that are native to Africa and South America. Hot-blooded bulbs. They could not survive outdoors in the winter in my climate, but if properly stored and restarted, they would multiply and bloom again.

This new world of bulbs required bending the old rules. I couldn't just put them in the ground in autumn and expect flowers in the spring; and getting them to bloom again turned out to be harder than getting a narcissus to bloom that second spring. I had to learn about artificially completing the life cycle of a tender bulb: they all need some sort of rest or drying period after flowering. When I had absorbed this lesson, I began to try other tender bulbs, with varied success. I learned I could fudge the rules and still be successful. For instance, *Crinum × powelli* bloomed for me after the second year in pot not because I had dried it out thoroughly, but because I hadn't. Its persistence in remaining green into the next summer saved it from being put away and forgotten. I learned that in some cases I didn't actually have to dry the bulb out completely to rest it. I experimented on that poor crinum, withholding water or giving it more as a whim, and understanding took hold.

Eucomis. The miniature alba-flowered form.

*T*HIS BOOK is about saving you from the same fate. Or at least shortening it. My hope is that your first attempts won't be the same near-misses and utter failures mine were. Even so, not all failure is bad. Killing a few bulbs can give valuable, if hard-earned, lessons for future success.

Not all of my early bulbs came from

Sinningia speciosa, one of the gloxinia species.

the Cruickshank catalog. One day, while walking down the aisle of a large garden center, I stopped at a display of plants that looked like African violets with their floppy, velvety foliage, but their flowers were huge — much bigger than any violet. It was as though everything else in that greenhouse disappeared except for an angelic light shining on that display.

These were not ordinary flowers. They reminded me of Alice's hallucinogenic trip to Wonderland. Each 6-inch pot had a skirt of pointed leaves in the softest velvety green. They were topped with a dozen or so flat-faced tubular flowers 2 inches across that looked a little like foxgloves with their speckled throats and came in colors of richest scarlet, blue, and wine purple. Around their outer edges was a band of white. I had never seen such richness and depth of color. It was one of those formative experiences that guide future actions. Of course, I had to have one.

The sign said "Gloxinia." One of my all-purpose gardening books informed me that the species was a native of Brazil and loved a warm, moist atmosphere. Gloxinias could not be easily grown on my windowsill, but they thrived under fluorescent lights. I found a warm spot, enclosed my fluorescents in a tent of clear plastic, and presto, I was a gloxinia grower.

The main problem I faced was that useful information about growing tender bulbs was hard to find. Read a handful of general bulb books and you will probably be most impressed by the equivocation and generalizations used in describing culture. True, it's hard to get specific about local conditions. But tender bulbs are easy to grow if you treat them right. Remember: the emphasis is on *tender*. Rule Number One is don't leave them outside in the winter if you want to see them next spring.

Following this cardinal rule is a pleasure. It forces me to live with my tender bulbs. They lounge around me on my cedar deck throughout the summer when many of them come into bloom, or bask on my sunny patio, waiting for their turn on stage. In winter I use my kitchen greenhouse window to encourage varieties, like hippeastrum, which most gardeners know as amaryllis. That's their time to shine. These are bulbs I've collected over the years, and they rebloom every winter around Christmas. Many are old crosses, not meriting even a glance these days by jaded gardeners. New varieties, including spectacular colors in double-flower forms, are appearing in catalogs each year. But I like bringing the old varieties back, even if they are not the best anymore.

They are old familiar friends and excellent practice for my bulb-growing skills.

I still have a soft spot for the mysterious veltheimias, which grow just as easily as amaryllis. With their wavy, dark and shiny leaves and dense clusters of tubular flowers in dusty pinks and yellows, they were my introduction to the fabulous world of South African bulbs. From a seemingly infinite variety of gladiolus to the small winsome blooms that appear between my flagstones in summer, South Africa is a rich treasure house of tender bulbs. This is where freesias come from and, although not nearly as well regarded as they were in the nineteenth century, a freesia will still make my nose twitch with excitement if I happen to be passing by a blooming specimen.

What's in store for someone just starting out in the world of tender bulbs? A glorious future. There are more new things to try than ever before. We are getting new crosses and hybrids that are bound to improve the whole bulb kingdom. I predict that some day, bulbs such as sprekelia will be as commonly grown as tulips. They are easily as beautiful, with their orchidlike carmine flowers perched singly above the curved spears of green foliage. *Sprekelia formosissima* has been known to horticulture as Aztec lily since the late 1500s, when they were introduced to Europe from Mexico. They are now commonly available and make excellent pot plants. Like the shy student at the high school dance, all they need is for someone to notice them.

I didn't realize until I was an adult how important fifth grade is in developing our futures. Without that little winter bulb project, who knows how long it would have taken to discover this fascinating aspect of gardening. I don't know if Miss Sharpley was a gardener herself, but she was a very good teacher.

Chapter 2

The Anatomy of a Bulb

W HAT MAKES BULBS UNIQUE? FOR STARTERS, THERE IS NO other plant that arrives complete with all its parts already present in the package. Leaves, flowers, base plate, and often the bud of a new bulb, are visible in embryo in the bulb. The whole package is neatly wrapped in a waterproof tunic. This characteristic of compacted essence has always given bulbs a uniquely privileged place in the hierarchy of plants. Besides their startling beauty, cures for a variety of real and imaginary diseases were attributed to them. And they still are in many societies, as Alice Biemond illustrates in this passage from a vivid memoir of her life on a farm in the Botswana bushveld, home for many of the most striking tender bulbs we grow today:

> Sina, the traditional herbalist woman, invited me for a chat in her consulting clay wall grass roof hut. On the entrance door lintel is a umbaza, *Ornithogalum longibracteum,* bulb to protect her house against evil spirits. Many dried healing herbs are powdered and stored in rows of small glass bottles which stand on boxes, shelves, and on the floor. Roots are drying in baskets. Sina knows each and everyone's cures for illnesses and African floral concoctions, which for instance, rapidly cure influenza without danger. Bulbs used for treatment and non-toxic medicines include: *Bowiea,*

Crinum jagus, an uncommon member of its tribe.

Gladiolus, Dietes, Drimia, Crinum, Haemanthus, Agapanthus, Bulbine, Boophane, Zantedaschia. In nature they grow in our southern African bushveld, forests and fields to be sacrificed for the benefit of mankind.

Readily transportable, bulbs could be slipped into a pocket and carried long distances, ready to regenerate themselves, much more quickly than seeds, simply by being dropped into the ground and watered. As a result, gardeners have spread bulbs around the world.

Over the years, the meaning of the word *bulb* has expanded. The catchall term gardeners use today covers corms, tubers, rhizomes, and tuberous roots. Collectively, botanists call them *geophytes*. They are all grown with much the same general culture even though they often look different.

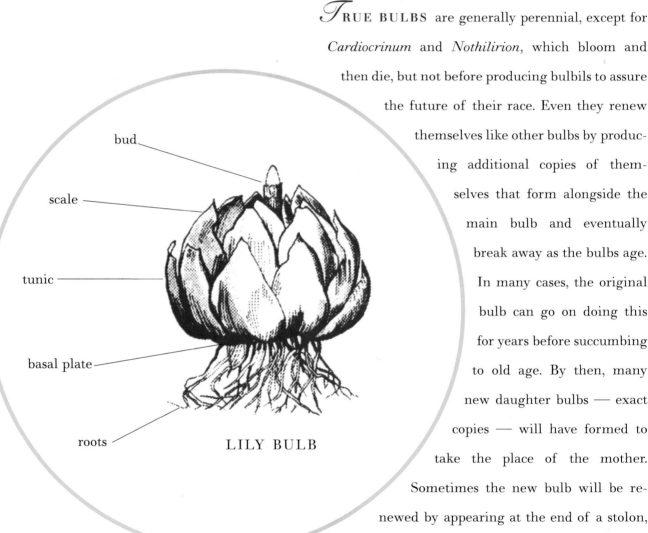

bud

scale

tunic

basal plate

roots

LILY BULB

*T*RUE BULBS are generally perennial, except for *Cardiocrinum* and *Nothilirion*, which bloom and then die, but not before producing bulbils to assure the future of their race. Even they renew themselves like other bulbs by producing additional copies of themselves that form alongside the main bulb and eventually break away as the bulbs age. In many cases, the original bulb can go on doing this for years before succumbing to old age. By then, many new daughter bulbs — exact copies — will have formed to take the place of the mother. Sometimes the new bulb will be renewed by appearing at the end of a stolon, an underground stem put out by the old bulb. The old bulb transfers its energy to the new bulb and then withers away. Some lilies do this, as well as some South African species.

$\mathcal{C}$ORMS look like bulbs but they don't renew themselves each year. They consist of a swelling of the fleshy base of the stem. This starchy, and sometimes tasty, stuff is used to nourish the plant over the summer. One genus, *Babiana*, was named because the first white settlers in Africa noticed the fondness baboons had for certain flowering bulbs, digging them up with gusto. Humans, too, have carried bulbs to eat, as well as to grow.

When nature wakes the corm, roots appear from a basal plate. The surface of the corm usually has a bud or two. As the plant uses up the starchy center of the corm, new corms begin to grow on the surface of the old one from those buds, leaving it withered and exhausted by the time flowers have appeared.

Aboveground, the leaves lengthen and mature until a bulge appears where the top leaves join. This is the flower head and it, too, continues to grow upward as the flower spike gets longer. The flower head separates into individual flower buds which eventually begin to color and bloom from the bottom of the flower spike up. Corms are represented by genera like acidanthera, gladiolus, and crocus.

GLADIOLUS

FREESIA

CANNA

$\mathcal{R}$HIZOMES look a bit like tubers but are really underground stems that carry buds and take many forms. They are considered a link between the tuber and the fleshy perennial root. Examples of rhizomes are achimenes, anemone, and zantedeschia.

TUBEROUS BEGONIA

RANUNCULUS

*T*UBERS differ from bulbs and corms in that they have no tunic or basal plate. The skin is often leathery, and roots can appear anywhere on their surface. Latent buds can also spring from anywhere on the surface. The buds begin as single leaves or stems that go on to produce flowers either singly or in clusters. Unlike corms or bulbs, tubers can be partially or entirely depleted during their growth cycle. Examples of these are begonia, gloxinia *(Sinningia)*, caladium, and cyclamen.

DAHLIA

*T*UBEROUS ROOTS are the final catchall category and are really just roots that have been modified through thickening. There are no buds on the root itself. The buds are found at the base of the stem, which is also the source of the top growth. The best known of these are dahlia, eremurus, and clivia. As you can see from the categories, you've probably already grown some tender bulbs without being aware of it.

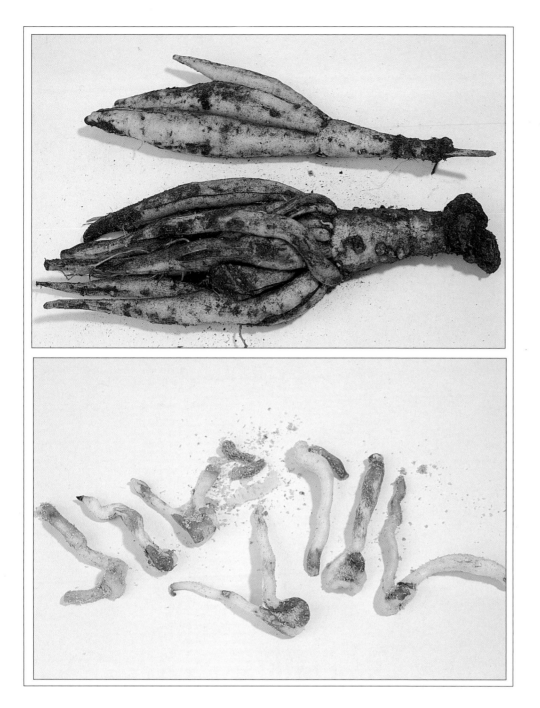

Incarvillea bulbs.

Sandersonia bulbs.

One of the pleasures of my early bulb education was opening the little paper sacks that bulbs come in. The variety of shapes and sizes always intrigued me, because there was no way to tell how they would look when they finally bloomed. The size of the bulb was no help. Small bulbs often produce huge blooms by comparison. Sometimes I didn't know which end was up, so I fudged by laying them down sideways. They always seemed to find the right way to grow. It was a small but important lesson in tender bulb culture: don't be put off by the small frustrations of form and function.

Chapter 3

Where Bulbs Come From

Whenever I show someone one of my tender bulbs in bloom, one of the first questions asked is inevitably, "Where does this come from?" This may sound like a naive, idle question, but it is a good starting point. Because, by asking where a bulb comes from, a gardener is taking a substantial step toward understanding the fundamentals of how to grow it.

When I started growing tender bulbs, the toughest concept for me to understand was how to adapt the infinite microclimates these bulbs come from to an ordinary home or yard. Where tender bulbs live in nature is unlike any home I would want to live in. Blistering hot days are followed by cool nights, and when the rainy season finally comes, it rains hard enough to flood their habitat completely. I've seen pictures of crinums in full bloom on a flooded plain where the water was a foot above the ground, lapping gently at the seemingly unconcerned stems.

Unfortunately, a lot of books on the subject are of little help. One volume on my shelf provides me with this information about a particularly tender bulb: "The bulbs should be planted 6–8 inches deep in June–July. During winter a covering of dry leaves or straw will give adequate protection from frost." What the writer doesn't say is that the advice applies to central and southern European growers for *Amaryllis belladonna*, a pretty but tricky bulb. In my part of the world, southern Ontario, in Canada, with a climate much like the northeastern

Winter-Growing versus Summer-Growing Bulbs

Tender bulbs come in both winter-rainfall and summer-rainfall versions. The winter version not only grows, but blooms then. It will probably be started into growth by the autumn. Foliage will form over early winter, and the flower spikes should show up shortly after. After flowering, the foliage should continue to grow but should have dried out by early summer. The pot is then put in a shaded, dry place. Examples of winter growers are most Cape bulbs, and the following: albuca, amaryllis, cyrtanthus, freesia, gloriosa (also summer-blooming), lachenalia, oxalis, ranunculus, veltheimia, watsonia, and *Zantedeschia aethiopica*.

Summer bloomers are planted in the spring. By May I have potted up acidanthera, alstroemeria, agapanthus, amarcrinum, canna, crinum, crocosmia, dahlia, eucomis, galtonia, gladiolus, gloriosa, haemanthus, hedychium, hemerocallis, ipoemia, lilium, nerine, ornithogalum, polianthes, sprekelia, tigridia, tulbaghia, and zantedeschia.

Both kinds of bloomers need good drainage when growing and a dry resting period when they are dormant. If these conditions are not met, the bulb will die.

(Opposite page 13): Oxalis deppei, Good luck leaf.

Nerine hybrids in many color varieties.

United States, this advice would necessitate a visit to the garden center next spring for a new bulb.

A lot of sorrow can be avoided by knowing the geographical home of your bulb's ancestors. Even then you can take heart. Like kids, tender bulbs have the endearing but frustrating quality of being able to survive in the darndest places.

*G*ENERALLY speaking, bulbs are divided into summer-rainfall and winter-rainfall types. "Rainfall" can cover both rain and snow. Many of the prettiest tender bulbs came from a Mediterranean climate. This is a general term that covers any climate of hot, dry summers and cool, wet winters. Plants experience a summer drought that is followed by rains during the winter, when most of the new growth is made.

Because of a combination of latitudes and mountain ranges around the world, the Mediterranean type of climate is not limited to the sea of the same name. If you look at a weather map of the world you will see that the Mediterranean climate can be found across an area at about 30 degrees latitude north and 30 degrees latitude south of the Equator. In the north, it includes the Mediterranean Sea's edge and the coast of California. South of the Equator, the Mediterranean climate passes through central Chile, the Cape Province of South Africa, and southwest and southern Australia. These parts of the world are the origin of our most desirable tender bulb species. The richest is South Africa, where more

Eucomis comosa. These are happy and regular summer bloomers in pots and can be planted outdoors for dramatic displays.

than 1,300 species have evolved. But there are other important bulb areas, too. Mexico has given us dahlias, sprekelia, and tigridia. South America is where hippeastrum (amaryllis), hymenocallis, gloxinia, and eucharis originate. Asia is home to many of our finest lilies. About the only place that doesn't have many bulbs is Australasia, although even there the Australian model of isolated groups of animals is duplicated with plants. Bulbs can be found there that are remotely related to those in other parts of the world. Botanists speculate that the continents separated before bulbs evolved sufficiently.

Since this is a book about tender bulbs, I will not dwell on Mediterranean bulbs such as tulips, narcissus, crocus, and scillas. They come from colder areas to the north. Those bulbs spend the summer in dormancy. But

come September or October, they begin to grow roots again. This is why we plant tulips in the autumn, to initiate the life cycle again at the appropriate time of year. Growth is stopped by the cold, to begin again once the warm, wet weather of spring arrives.

It's the area south of 30 degrees latitude that interests us. Here, the growing season is sparked, not

Dahlia 'Bishop of Liandaff'.

A harsh climate
brings out the best
in these Babianas.

by the warmth of spring, but by the autumn rains, and because winter is relatively warm, that is when the top growth appears, along with the flowers. All summer — a period of intense, dry heat — bulbs in this area lay dormant. There are often no leaves on the surface to show where flowers flourished a few months earlier, but below ground, the plants are very much alive. Using their sensitive root systems, they make decisions about whether or not they will bloom that year, especially if Mother Nature has mistreated them. Many tender bulbs will stay alive, underground, sometimes for years, waiting for their moment to bloom. There are many stories from plant hunters of sudden wet years producing extraordinary flower shows and in the process uncovering bulbs that hadn't been seen in an area in decades.

Tender bulbs' roots have other interesting functions. Sometimes, they will drag an improperly planted bulb a foot through solid earth to get to its ideal depth. Tender bulbs belie their name. Many grow in less-than-tender climates, with periods of torrential rain, followed by earth-baking heat and sunshine in what often appears to be solid-as-brick clay. Yet these same bulbs will often accommodate themselves to much less rigorous pot culture. The secret is in playing the climate game. Be tough. Be harsh. Just don't let them freeze. And since bulb growing, like all gardening, is an art that depends on the acquisition and application of constantly learned skills, every time you succeed with a particular species, you'll increase your confidence in the growing of all bulbs.

Chapter 4

Lessons of the Amaryllis

MANY GARDENERS GET INTRODUCED TO THE WORLD OF HOT-blooded tender bulbs without even knowing it. Who hasn't grown at least one amaryllis? People give them as gifts. Even the smallest supermarkets carry amaryllis in their vegetable and flower section in late autumn, often with the instruction to "Just add water." They bloom at Christmas. They were the first exotic tender bulbs I tried growing in a pot. I still grow them every year. Despite their ubiquity — or maybe because of it — there is no better plant to start on than amaryllis when you are learning the secrets of growing tender bulbs.

After you've had success with tender bulbs, you may find your voice taking on a scoffing tone when talking about the gaudy amaryllis, whose scientific name is really *Hippeastrum*. Which is too bad. Amaryllis suffer from an image problem that no longer applies to the group. When I first started growing them, some 20 years ago, they came in a kind of rusty orange color with no frills. Just three or four big trumpet-shaped flowers, 6 inches across, on a foot-high fleshy stem. These days they not only have frills, but you can get double-flowered varieties, stripes, and picotees (a pencil-line of contrasting color, usually red on the edge of the petals). There are deep true reds and the dustiest rose colors imaginable, along with miniature yellows and a variety called 'Papillio' that looks like it was collected in a jungle in Brazil. All are well worth growing, and once you have mastered an amaryllis you are ready for almost any tender bulb.

(Page 18):
Amaryllis in bloom.

Amaryllis bulb with off-set ready to pot in a 6- to 8-inch pot with top third of the bulb above the surface of the soil.

My first attempts at blooming and (here's the trick) reblooming an amaryllis resulted in failure. I dutifully followed the regular advice: after the bulb blooms, keep the leaves growing until somehow, magically, they were supposed to die down and I was to store the bulb, pot and all, for two months and then resurrect the pot, simply watering again, and wait for my flowers. It didn't happen the way the instructions that came with the amaryllis said it would. First of all, the bulb was smaller the second time around, and second, I had fewer flowers. Only three small flowers on one stem, compared to four on each of two stems the first time. I knew I was doing something wrong.

Over the years, I learned the secrets of growing amaryllis to get perfect bulbs every time. Start with a pot that accommodates the bulb with just an inch

or so of space around its "waistline." The pot can be plastic or clay, but it should be at least 6 or 7 inches tall. It's a good idea to put stones in the bottom inch or so to give the bottom some weight when the long and heavy flower stalk takes off. Fill under and around the bulb with bagged potting soil from the garden center. The bulb should sit about one-third of the way out of the pot. Water thoroughly, put the pot in a warm and shaded spot, and don't water again until the soil is dry to the touch.

Make sure watering doesn't outpace root growth. It is critical to water and let the pot dry out before carefully watering again. This is an important rule for any bulb being started in a pot from a dry state. Once growth appears, fertilize when watering, at about half the strength recommended on the package. About eight weeks later you will have at

The vivid colors of this *Hippeastrum papillo* show why this form is one of the most popular available.

least four single or double trumpet-shaped flowers up to 8 inches across that can be the centerpiece of a windowsill for at least a couple of weeks during the coldest months of the year. Sometimes the bulb repeats the flowering feat again a few weeks later. Who could not love the amaryllis?

Aftercare is important for good flowering the second time around. This is where the inexperienced grower usually falls down. To get around this problem, I let Mother Nature take over. I plant the bulbs outdoors in the summer. Amaryllis flowers are followed by three or four long strap-shaped leaves. These leaves should be permitted to grow in a pot in a bright indoor environment until all danger of frost has passed. In early summer, about the time beans are planted, I take the bulbs out of their pots and drop them, with as little disturbance to the roots as possible, into a prepared hole in the garden. By "prepared" I mean that I put a couple of inches of compost and some dry fertilizer in the bottom of the hole. Then I bury the bulb up to where the leaves begin.

Once the bulbs are settled outdoors, I like to cut some leafy tree branches and put them into the ground around the plants so the leaves get plenty of shade at first. I feed and water the bulbs regularly and allow them to grow all summer until the end of August, when I pull them out and let them dry in the sun for a few hours before putting them on old newspapers in a dark, warm, dry place, in my case the basement, for at least two months. After the first month I cut off the now dry and brittle leaves, but I leave the roots alone. By November or December the amaryllis bulbs are ready to be restarted again for blooms at Christmas and beyond. If everything has worked correctly, many will already have flower buds pushing out through the top.

Amaryllis is supposed to be foolproof, and it is . . . up to a point. Without proper aftercare, the second year's flowering can be disappointing. A neighbor of mine proudly displays an amaryllis in leaf in her front window all year round and has done so for years. It appears never to have gone into dormancy, or bloomed again. What went wrong? Keeping a bulb like amaryllis in a pot year after year can't be a good idea. Nutrients are limited by the size of the pot even if fertilizer is applied regularly. I found that when I gave my amaryllis a regular outdoor vacation in the ground they became better bulbs.

Little effort is required to bloom an amaryllis as well as this.

Chapter 5

Planting and Growing Tender Bulbs

How Tender Bulbs Grow

One of the oddest bulbs to grace this planet is a shy specimen from the Cape of Good Hope that goes by the local name of kukumakranka. You can look it up under the Latin name *Gethyllis*, which itself derives from the Greek word for leek. It does look like a leek — from outer space — when growing. The part above the surface of the earth has a sort of white zebra-striped stem encircled with rings of green hairlike growths, all topped with up to 20 chivelike leaves. That's not the odd part, though. The odd part is the fruit that follows the single, nondescript flower. It comes out of the ground next to the stem looking like a club-shaped orange-colored finger with semitransparent skin. The fruit is said to taste like a cross between pineapple and banana. Kukumakranka is living proof that when it comes to tender bulbs, fiction is hard-put to outguess reality.

Despite the life cycle of *Gethyllis*, growing bulbs is like growing anything in soil: a matter of understanding the necessary conditions for the plant to thrive, and applying the proper culture. Remember that climate is the overriding influence on a bulb's life. It's why a bulb can be totally dormant for months and even years, but if suddenly it rains, the plant leaps into life almost instantly.

Moisture control is very important in tender bulb culture because most of them come from an environment that is typified by extended rainy and then dry periods. The bulbs evolved to survive periods of drought by having surface foliage that simply withers under the relentlessly beating sun. Below ground, the bulbs rest cool and expectant, waiting for the first drops of moisture to prompt an emerging shoot that will begin the bulb's aboveground life again.

*W*HEN my bulbs are in full and rampant growth they cannot seem to get enough food and water. I pour on the fertilizer and water daily if the plants are in constant sun. Even bulbs that seem to get no food at all in their natural habitat, stuck in some rock cleft in the blazing sun of Cape Province, do better when fed regularly at this stage, especially if pot-grown.

In its natural setting, a bulb's life cycle begins with the rains. In the Northern Hemisphere, that is spring. It's when we see the results of last autumn's outdoor plantings and when we get our prettiest show of the year. In the Southern Hemisphere, the same phenomenon is duplicated in the autumn. In the Southern Hemisphere, summer functions like our winter, in that both shut down plant growth. Here it is because of freezing temperatures. There, growth stops because of harsh conditions of the other extreme: relentless heat and drought.

Hardy bulbs start their life cycle in our autumn with root growth, then stop during the cold winter months. But they begin growing again once spring comes, usually blooming right away, to be followed

(Opposite page 25): Crocosmia 'Lucifer' in garden bed with *Lily* 'Triptique' and *Euphorbia carniolica* offers a combination with four to six weeks' flowering each summer.

(Below): Seedlings and larger bulbs thriving in midsummer on a shaded deck.

by rampant production of leaves and then dormancy before the cycle begins again. Tender bulbs follow essentially the same cycle, only reversed. Think of their autumn as our spring.

For tender bulbs, the annual rest period is so important that bulbs won't flower next year if they don't get one. I don't water my bulbs when they are beginning their rest period in the same way I do when they are in full summer growth. In fact, I don't water them at all. The plants let me know when this time comes by slowing their growth and showing a little less vigor.

The trouble with some bulbs is that they don't know they should stop growing. That's when I have to step in and take matters into my own hands. I immediately cut back on both fertilizer and water. It should take less than a month before I've cut off watering altogether, letting the leaves grow limp before snipping them off and tucking the pot, soil and all, under a basement bench indoors where the temperature never goes much below 50°F.

I like to leave most bulbs in their pots during the rest period because the roots remain undisturbed. Bulbs seem to shrivel and dry out in home conditions sooner if they lose their soil-covered root ball, and for me offsets stand a better chance of survival if they stay attached to the main bulb in a pot until I am ready to restart growth. Also, a number of bulbs send their stolons (a form of stem that forms one or more new plants), if they have them, out to considerable distances, and disturbing them can cause setbacks to the bulbs.

The way I store tender bulbs grown directly in the garden, such as many of the gladiolus, is without soil attached, digging them up and letting them dry off for a few days before cutting off the stems. It's good to store them in dry peat. With pot-grown bulbs, I usually leave the bulb in the soil during the entire drying-out period. In spring it's easy enough to shake off the dusty surface soil or dump out the lot and add new compost. You could decide you'd like to abandon the pot and try them in that sunny spot in the border, for a change. Go ahead. I've had very good luck predigging a hole and filling it with rich topsoil before putting a prestarted bulb in and watering generously. Plants often bloom longer and produce larger bulbs by the end of the growing season if they are grown in prepared soil outdoors.

I HESITATE to say this, because most books caution bulb growers not to water during the dormancy period, but in our modern homes, with their overheated basements in the winter, if you don't water you risk the chance of some of your bulbs totally drying out and dying during the dormant period. I've had bulbs just shrivel up and disappear. If, a couple of months after I put them in my dark, warm storage area, my pots are light to the touch and obviously bone dry, I will water the pots lightly, just enough to keep the bulbs from shriveling. This can be confusing at first, and it must be done with the utmost care to prevent the passing on of mixed messages to your bulbs. What I usually do is err on the side of not adding water. The fact is, too much water will hurt the bulbs, virtually guaranteeing that they won't flower the next year. Many bulbs need a baking-off period to flower reliably. Remember, in their natural state, some can remain dormant for years, waiting to pop up. I know how difficult it is to keep from watering, but when sympathy calls on me to be less cruel, I take comfort in the words of A.T. de Villiers, a well-known South African writer on the bulbs of his country:

"The possibility that there is, as it were, a sort of 'soup of life' seething beneath the surface of this region could not but be enhanced by the phenomenon of 1990. Ordinarily, the drought of summer breaks in the autumnal rains of April. The hidden bulbs and corms begin to burgeon, coming to flower from May onwards but mostly in late August and September, in the spring. In 1990 the April rains were the heaviest and most prolonged since records were first kept in 1856. The seasonal pools filled up quickly and every hollow became a pool. The winter rains maintained the high water table and it was not until

September that the hollows began to drain and the seasonal pools to retract to their usual high level marks. Reports began to come in of new species found, of color varieties known in the literature but very seldom seen, of species appearing where they had not previously been found."

As a general rule, it's a good idea to ease off on the watering in any bulb when the plant is at the end of its growth cycle. The leaves will be full but beginning to turn brown here and there. The bulb, if you can see it, will have stopped increasing in size and will have a nice big shape for its type, and just look and feel healthy. Don't be afraid to dig your finger into the soil of your pots and feel how hard your bulbs are. This will tell you a lot about their health. If they feel as hard as onions in autumn, they are good. Any show of softness means you are doing something wrong.

If you grow your tender bulbs in containers, don't hesitate to repot at any time of the year, except the dormant period. Pot-grown bulbs may put on a burst of speed in a particularly good summer and by July, in my climate, are bursting out of their containers. Without disturbing the roots, I give them a pot one size larger even though they may be near their time for a dormant rest.

Some bulbs, like *Sprekelia formossisima* and *Eucharis grandiflora*, should never be dried off completely, but can be induced to flower more than once a year by reducing water, growing the plant in dryer conditions for a month or two, then starting gradually to water again. This usually works best when they are growing in warmer climates than mine.

Some of the most desirable summer bulbs never seem to forget that their natural growing season is

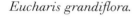

Eucharis grandiflora.

Growing Bulbs Indoors

What is the secret of growing tender bulbs indoors, I hear you ask? Is it the watering? The dormancy period? Do I feed, or don't I? Should I put my pots outdoors in the summer, or should I rigidly control them like a college experiment? Relax, my fellow gardeners. Don't brood on the specifics. Look at the big picture. The secret to growing tender bulbs in pots permanently is to know whether they have annual roots or perennial roots.

Annual-rooted bulbs include tuberous begonias, gloxinias, caladiums, lachenalias, freesias, and gladiolus, among others. They all lose their roots at the end of the growing season. The leaves die down in preparation for the beginning of the dormant period. In nature, they are kept very dry by their habitat, which usually parches up between wet seasons. I find that it's a good idea not to leave these to dry out in pots if I want to control their flowering time because they will invariably sprout at the first hint of moisture at an inappropriate moment in this gardener's imaginary schedule.

Because these bulbs follow a seasonal rhythm, I like to plant them so that they follow the rhythm of my seasons. After planting, water the pots generously and allow them to almost dry out between waterings until foliage begins to grow. Encourage root growth to fill the pot, but don't kill it with too much water at first. Once foliage is growing well, almost no amount of water seems too much if conditions are bright for the foliage. Once flowering occurs, the foliage will begin to deteriorate; that's the signal to reduce watering so that the soil is allowed to dry out for short periods. Once the foliage is dying down, stop watering completely and allow the bulbs to ripen in a warm but shady spot for a few days before cutting off their foliage. Store the bulbs in brown grocery bags with the name written on the side, or in the cut-off legs of an old pair of panty hose with last year's label.

Confusion often comes over when to plant. Natives of South Africa begin their growth period in the fall, and that's when they should be repotted. They rest in summer. There are others, like gloxinias, fancy-leaved caladiums, and some of the oxalis, that are dormant in winter but start growing in spring. They should be given fresh soil and moisture at that time.

Growing perennial-rooted bulbs in pots requires a different kind of psychology. Don't remove them from their pots except to pot them in bigger pots, once they have grown into clumps. Not disturbing the roots is key. Instead, add enriched, fresh soil to the surface at the beginning of each growing season for these bulbs, which are often quite long-lived — half a dozen years, or more. Some, such as clivia, eucharis, agapanthus, and some of the crinums, are evergreen. These have semidry periods when watering should be reduced, but they should never be allowed to dry out completely.

Some perennial-rooted bulbs lose their leaves during the dormant season. They include hippeastrum (amaryllis), nerine, eucomis, and some haemanthus. I store these in the soil in which they are planted, keeping it just moist enough to keep the roots from drying out. Nerine likes cooler, dryer conditions than the others, but the essential key is finding the balance that keeps the roots from drying out too fast. If that happens, the soil in the pot can be judiciously watered once a month during dormancy to keep the roots plump.

Potting Summer Bulbs

BULB NAME	PLANTING CALENDAR	TIME UNTIL FLOWERS	TIME IN BLOOM
Achimenes	Feb.–March	8 weeks	2–3 months
Acidanthera	April–May	15 weeks	3 weeks
Agapanthus	March–April	12 weeks	2–3 months
Alstroemeria	March–April	10 weeks	2 months
Amarcrinum	April–May	15 weeks	4 weeks
Amaryllis belladonna	Aug.–Sept.	9 months	3 weeks
Begonia	Feb.–March	10 weeks	4 months
Canna	March–May	12 weeks	2 months
Crinum	April–May	15 weeks	3 weeks
Dahlia	April–May	14 weeks	2 months
Dierama	Oct.–Nov.	9 months	4 weeks
Eucharis	April–May	1–12 months	3 weeks
Eucomis	April–May	12 weeks	2 months
Freesia	July–Aug.	4 months	1 month
Galtonia	April–May	12 weeks	1 month
Gladiolus	April–May	12 weeks	1 month
Gloriosa	Jan.–March	5 months	2 months
Habranthus	Oct.–Nov.	8 months	2 weeks
Haemanthus	March–May	14 weeks	5 weeks
Hedychium	March–April	16 weeks	6 weeks
Hippeastrum	Oct.–April	12 weeks	2–3 months
Homeria	Sept.–Oct.	8 months	3 weeks
Hymenocallis	April–May	10 weeks	3 weeks
Ipheion	Oct.–Nov.	6 months	3 weeks

BULB NAME	PLANTING CALENDAR	TIME UNTIL FLOWERS	TIME IN BLOOM
Ixia	Oct.–Nov.	6 months	3 weeks
Lachenalia	Aug.–Sept.	6 months	1 month
Lilium	April–May	10 weeks	3 weeks
Lycoris	Aug.–Sept.	10 months	4 weeks
Moraea	April	2–8 months	1 month
Nerine	March–May	4 months	1 month
Ornithogalum	March–May	14 weeks	6 weeks
Oxalis	Sept.–Nov.	8 weeks	variable
Polianthes	April–May	20 weeks	4 weeks
Ranunculus	March–April	5 months	5 weeks
Rhodohypoxis	April–May	4 weeks	4 weeks
Romulea	Sept.–Oct.	5 months	4 weeks
Sandersonia	April	12 weeks	4 weeks
Scadoxus	March–May	16 weeks	3 weeks
Sparaxis	November	8 months	4 weeks
Sprekelia	April	8 weeks	2–3 weeks
Tecophilaea	Sept.–Oct.	8 months	2 weeks
Tigridia	March–April	12 weeks	1 month
Tritonia	Sept.	8 months	1 month
Tulbaghia	April	16 weeks	4–6 weeks
Vallota	June	8 weeks	1 month
Veltheimia	Sept.	5 months	4–6 weeks
Watsonia	April–May	16 weeks	1 month
Zantedeschia	March–April	8–10 weeks	5–7 weeks
Zephyranthes	March–April	16 weeks	3–5 weeks

the opposite of our own. We may plant them in spring to grow in our summer, but they really want to bloom in our winter and will try to revert to their natural growth cycle. To survive, they have to be lifted in the autumn and kept dry over the winter, to be planted again in the spring. Most South African bulbs are too tender to survive outdoors in the winter in North America except in places like California and the southeastern states. I grow mine in pots all year or first in pots for indoor pleasures, then I put them in the garden in the summer and store them indoors for the winter to be started in a pot again after a two-month dormancy. Above all else, remember that a tender bulb will not tolerate temperatures below freezing. Half-hardy bulbs can stand some frost but won't survive long periods of it. And even hardy bulbs will die if frozen and thawed too quickly and subjected to wet conditions during dormancy.

ℋOW TO PLANT AND GROW TENDER BULBS

When I first got serious about bulbs, my strategy was to buy a bag of everything the store had available, from *Acidanthera* to *Zephyranthes*.

When the spring shipment arrived, I literally went from bin to bin, taking a few of these, some of those and one of these (the expensive ones). I planted as soon as I could work the ground. Virtually all of my acquisitions came up. Some bloomed, and some didn't, but I soon got the idea of what to try again. The point of my experiment was to try to grow summer bulbs among my other flowers in the beds in my garden, but I soon learned that they like a place of their own, far from the competitive roots of nearby herbaceous plants.

This meant I had to find one spot in my garden

Acidanthera bicolor has been placed in the gladiolus tribe. Let's hope its many charms do not get lost to growers in such a huge crowd.

just right for bulbs. It turned out to be a sand-filled section that received sun almost all day. I boosted the sand with compost dug in during the spring before I put down my bulbs. They liked the quick-draining, rich soil that warmed up quickly and stayed that way because it was beside a small sunny patio covered in flat sandstone slabs. Most of the bulbs thrived, and I saved the survivors in paper bags and replanted them the next spring. It was a very instructive exercise. I found out what I could grow well and discovered the needs of the temperamental bulbs I knew only by name from the literature I could find.

Those of us with south-facing gentle slopes can plant many summer bulbs in the nooks and crannies of a rock garden. This is the traditional method of dealing with them outdoors, and it works beautifully as long as they have no competition from herbaceous plants and annuals. Clumps here and there, particularly when they are toasted by the summer sun, can increase supplies in no time. But this approach presents a problem when it's time to take them out of the ground, before the frost comes. I must confess that I find the prospect of spending early autumn afternoons digging in search of pea-sized bulbs such as romulea or rhodohypoxis daunting.

Most committed bulb growers take the luck out of real-estate location by planting tender bulbs in specially prepared raised beds. These can be made from railway ties, concrete blocks, or actual rocks. The bottom 6 inches can be filled with rubble and a gravel mix. Another foot of 50-50 compost and sand/pea gravel mixture will give perfect drainage and is ideal for any bulb.

It's a good idea to plant bulbs as soon as you get them. This begins the all-important root growth that ideally precedes the top growth. I avoid already-sprouted bulbs if I can. But

Tuberous begonias ready for planting in individual 4- to 6-inch pots.

Begonia tuberhybrida. One of the most hybridized tender
bulbs there is. Its ancestors are lost in the mists of time.

if they have sprouted, I plant them anyway: nothing
ventured nothing gained. Outdoors, the planting
hole is prepared according to the needs of the species
I am trying. Usually I just mix some compost in with
the soil that is already there and sprinkle the hole
with some bone meal. There are also boxed chemical fertilizer compounds made especially for bulbs. If
I am worried about the ground getting too wet for
the bulbs, I pour in a few inches of pure sand on top
of the compost layer and plant the bulbs right on the
sand, surrounding them with more sand so the
drainage will be as perfect as possible. Good
drainage is an important consideration for all bulbs.

For easy handling, I prefer to grow most of my
summer bulbs in pots, rather than directly in the
garden. Even if a bulb is eventually destined for the

flower bed, I often start it in a pit and plant the root
ball in the garden when the weather warms sufficiently. Pots allow me to give that intimate care most
tender bulbs demand during the winter. With this in
mind, I start with my own custom-made soil. My
mix these days is usually made up from things I have
on hand. I usually make up a big batch in a wheel-
barrow and then bag it for later use. I start with
homemade compost from my garden composter, or I
use bagged, high-quality potting soil. I've also used
some of the commercial soilless mixes such as Pro-
Mix, which are peat-based. Just by themselves they
make excellent starter mixes to promote root
growth.

To the compost I add the coarsest sand I can find
at my builder's supply so the proportions are about

My Window Greenhouse

My window greenhouse is my most valuable growing asset. In the space of an area 30 inches deep, 33 inches wide, and 6 feet high, I grow a variety of plants—such as alstroemeria, oxalis, and hymenocallis—that take full advantage of the best sun because the space juts out from the east side of my house. By using wire shelves on several levels, I can easily grow 50 or more plants in the space of an ordinary window. I cover the front with a hanging Plexiglas sheet to contain humidity and have a small muffin fan circulating air inside. In the summer I cover the outside with greenhouse shade cloth. A customized galvanized metal tray I had made contains stones and gravel to maintain high humidity. You'll grow anything in this setup.

Only curious squirrels and nimble-footed raccoons are likely to disturb this seedling nursery area on a shaded deck.

50-50. Into this go three or four cups of powdered rock. Powdered rock is a wonderful ingredient that's not used often enough these days because chemical fertilizers are supposed to be easier. Powdered rock is a natural, nonburning ingredient in most of the soils of the world, but what it does to fertility in a bulb-growing situation is totally out of proportion to its chemical analysis. Beyond this point I can only suggest that some gardeners add tiny charcoal pieces to sweeten the soil, or larger stones to coarsen the mixture. This is the custom-made part of the exercise, but the most important consideration for good drainage.

For tender bulbs grown indoors, 8-inch pots are fine, but outdoors I like bigger containers: pots a foot in diameter are not too big. Small ones dry out quickly, particularly if they are made of clay, and big

bulbs, like crinum, don't have the leg room in a small pot to develop a good set of roots. When a pot stands outside all summer in the open it needs plenty of watering. Every day is not too often in some cases. This is one place where plastic pots can prove superior to other more porous kinds. If I have a number of clay pots outside I bunch them together in the growing area, and the soil seems to stay moist longer.

I fill the bottom of each pot with coarse gravel to give it a nontippable base to counterbalance eventual lush growth. Some tender bulbs, such as tuberous anemones and cyclamen, need to be on or near the surface in moist compost. Stem rooters, such as lilies, may need more depth, like 6 to 8 inches of soil.

Depending on how soon I want my potted bulbs to bloom, I put them in a cool area to prevent them from flowering too early, or in a warm, bright place

Some essential ingredients of a bulb potting mix. (From top left): 1) commercial soilless mix, 2) sand, 3) bulbs ready for a covering, 4) vermiculite, 5) silver sand, 6) perlite.

and watch them flower, usually shortly after planting. One of the pleasures of summer bulbs in containers is that I can control the show, somewhat, by retarding growth in this way. Of course, with summer bulbs I never want it too cool. Forty-five degrees Fahrenheit is plenty low to be on the safe side, with these bulbs. To maintain proper temperatures, large herbaceous perennials can surround a patch of tender bulbs in the middle of a bed. I've often sunk pots of summer bloomers right into the ground of my beds, particularly when potted in clay, to retain moisture and keep the roots cool. The plant benefits from an outdoor regime, and the bulbs remain cool, with root systems that grow extremely thick.

Most bulb growers have both tender and hardy bulbs in their collections. Because they demand opposite watering and dormant periods, the two kinds should not be grown in the same outdoor bed. Lifting the summer grower (for instance, gladiolus) for inside dormancy will disturb the new root growth of the autumn-winter grower (like tulips) planted nearby and will probably put an end to its spring flower show.

Once you've grown your tender bulbs into rich clumps that bloom at the top of their form, you'll have passed one of the tests given to applicants seeking the head gardenership on a nineteenth-century estate. There's a kind of horticultural majesty in the stately procession of blooming in tender bulbs from summer through winter that caught the fancy of Victorian gardeners. Those of us still in the apprenticeship stage can look forward to many happy hours of discovery.

Chapter 6

Where to Get Tender Bulbs

$\mathcal{E}$VER SINCE THE FLEMISH DIPLOMAT OGIER GHISLAIN de Busbeq smuggled some bulbs to the Imperial collection in Vienna from his posting as Ambassador to the Ottoman Empire in 1554, and thereby introduced tulips to Europe, gardeners have been devising ways to get more bulbs, not all of them aboveboard. So rare were those early tulips that the entire Imperial collection was itself stolen when its keeper, the eminent Charles d'Ecluse (Clusius) accepted a post as a botany professor in Holland. He had set such a high price on the new bulbs that someone crept into his garden one night and took them all. Tulips soon began to appear all over Holland — presumably the bulbs and offsets of the stolen booty — and that, eventually, is how the Dutch bulb industry came into being. Gardeners have always liked their bulbs rare and hard to get and have been willing to pay for them. One way or another.

In the past, many bulbs were simply dug up in their wild state and shipped off by local entrepreneurs who saw the opportunity for quick profit in a countryside with very few other opportunities. The practice is frowned on these days, and permits to dig are needed almost everywhere rare bulbs exist. Still, more interesting rare bulb varieties are available today than ever before. I'm convinced this is because of dedicated hobbyists who see clearly the need to save plant species threatened by humanity's need to expand into new territories.

When I first started growing tender bulbs, a couple of decades ago, I had to

A typical commercially packaged summer bulb mix available from many garden centers.

(Opposite p. 39):
Sinningia speciosa, one
of the gloxinia species.

be as diligent as a latter-day Ogier Ghislain de Bus-beq in obtaining unusual specimens. Now it's as easy as filling out an order form and waiting for the mail-man to arrive with my selections. But buying any sort of bulb can still be a hit-or-miss proposition. I am dependent on my suppliers for getting good stock in the first place, storing it properly, and shipping it so it doesn't arrive at my house shriveled or spotted with gray mold.

There are several ways to get the bulbs you want. You can go to the local garden center, usually in late winter or early spring, and choose from what they have. My local center has open boxes of bulbs covered with what I call gardeners' pornography: at-tractive photographs of perfect flowers blooming in a natural setting. But it's the condition of the drab-looking bulbs that should catch the purchaser's eye. The best bulbs are plump, full, and unshriveled. No sprouted ends are allowed unless you simply must have those particular bulbs and are willing to risk their death in order to possess them.

Importing bulbs from abroad sometimes involves getting government-issued sanitary certificates, or bills of good health that are handed out by the Department of Agriculture of the exporting and importing countries under a complicated international agreement, called by its acronym CITES, that covers the export of endangered species. But don't be put off. Most of the tender bulbs discussed in this book are not affected by such strictures. Even the rarest tender bulbs are increasingly becoming available as nursery-grown stock from hand-collected seeds. Or as seeds themselves, which can cross borders without officially issued bills of health.

Ordering from a bulb catalog can be as simple as checking off a few marks on a form, or it can be a big mental hurdle. All those names in the catalog, mostly in Latin, can be daunting. I suggest placing a small order at first. You'll know soon enough if you would make another purchase from that particular firm. As for the Latin, it will be tripping off your tongue in no time. The back half of this book consists of an alphabetical listing of the most grower-friendly bulbs from my experience. I have also included a large list of mail-order bulb sources.

For those gardeners fortunate enough to have a bulb seller near them, it's best to order from a local firm to guarantee early delivery. For similar reasons, if I want to procure the best bulbs, I get to the garden center as soon as the shipment arrives and root

Seeds are folded in tinfoil packets with the name typed on a tag on the packet. Thin Styrofoam sheets protect the seeds in the mailing envelope.

How to Import Plants

Someday you may want to import your own bulbs or seeds. Seeds are normally free from import restrictions, but plants and bulbs are not. You will need an import permit label.

To check their entry status
in the United States, write:

Permit Unit
Plant Protection and Quarantine
Animal and Plant Inspection Service
U.S. Department of Agriculture
638 Federal Building
Hyattsville, MD 20782

For Canadian permits write:

Agriculture Canada
Plant Protection Division
150 Bridgeland Avenue
Toronto
M6A 3A6

---

through the bins for the firmest I can find. However, even the largest general-interest garden centers have only the best-known bulbs and likely no knowledgeable staff.

Local and national rock garden societies are an excellent way of connecting to bulb growers near you. Starting one locally could bring some of those closet bulb growers out into the open.

A final source of bulbs is friends. This can be a good or bad thing, depending on the skill of the friend. If he has an overabundance of bulbs, follow his growing instructions carefully. If the bulb he gives you was once large and is now getting smaller each year, save yourself some heartache and throw it out. Rescuing ailing plants takes a few years and considerable dedication that could probably be better employed learning to grow healthy new varieties you've never tried before.

I used to see tender bulbs arrive in the early spring, but many catalogs nowadays list some during every season. Selecting tender bulbs has now become a year-round challenge. And pleasure.

To increase the probability of hits over misses when trying new bulbs, here are some guidelines:

- Know where the bulbs you buy come from. This will help you in their cultivation, particularly if they need a long rest period.
- Climate gives important clues to cultivation.
- When choosing bulbs from a bin, remember that the best bulbs are plump, full, and unshriveled. There should be no sprouting and no gray, white, or black mold on the surface of the bulb.
- If there is even a touch of mold, treat the bulb with a commercial bulb dust containing both a fungicide and bactericide before planting.

Achimenes longiflora

Chapter 7

Increasing Your Supply

PROPAGATING FROM OFFSETS

The urge to propagate my own tender bulbs first struck when I sent away for a rare variety. After many weeks of waiting, I received a corm hardly big enough to cover my thumbnail. "This is what I paid $25 for?" I mused incredulously. Alas, most bulbs look best when they fill a pot with their stems, leaves, and flowers. I brooded darkly: at this rate it would take me hundreds of dollars to fill a single 8-inch pot. There had to be a better way. And there was: I started to grow my own.

Propagating bulbs is not limited to the common approach of putting one in the ground and hoping it grows well enough to produce offsets that will give a couple more bulbs the next year. Bulbs can also be started from seed. And, there are special techniques developed by the Dutch to make single bulbs produce an almost endless supply of perfect copies of themselves.

But the offset method is a good starting point. Crinum and amaryllis are examples of plants that develop offsets as the main bulb grows larger. The offsets gradually form clumps of smaller bulbs with their own leaves, and as long as a portion of the base plate is present on the bulb, it can be snapped off and will

Crinum moorei. The most common, soft pink form.

Gladiolus nanus mixed.

eventually grow into a new bulb exactly like the mother bulb. I usually wait until the end of the growing season before trying to separate bulbs. Some, like sprekelia, divide readily, but others, like the long-lived crinum, not only do not like to be disturbed, but will often sulk, growing slowly and hesitantly for up to three years before resuming what could be called normal growth.

Once the leaves have begun to get slack and brown, it is time to gently twist off the offsets. I take the plants out of the ground or pot and allow the bulb clump to dry in the sun until a shake loosens the dirt and permits a look at the base. Some offsets will be hanging on by a few threads. Those still firmly attached and growing out of the mother, even

though they have distinct leaf growths, should be left attached. After trimming the leaves off, I either repot with the nose of the bulb above the soil surface, or I store the clump dry and do my separating and dividing just before I want to repot, which will be some months in the future.

Corms, such as gladiolus or sparaxis, form new corms on top of the old ones, which gradually wither by the end of the growing season. One of the benefits of corms is that they produce cormels, immature bulbs that typically need a few years in the ground to grow large enough to produce a crop of flowers. Cormels are gathered at the end of the growing season when the flowering has finished and the leaves are beginning to wither. I dig the bulbs and let them dry on the ground in the sun for a few hours. The cormels will be lightly attached to the bulbs and will probably fall away as the soil dries out.

If I want new plants soon, I gather the cormels and dry them for a few weeks and then plant them in a tray of my regular potting soil, keeping the soil moist, but not soaking, over the winter. The cormels will sprout if they are ready. If not, they will remain dormant, and a cool room or a cold frame that remains dry and does not freeze is ideal for their winter rest. I grow sprouted cormels in a separate garden bed or in a wide pot, urging them on as quickly as possible by giving them plenty of light, moisture, and fertilizer. Growing immature bulbs together as a group, without the presence of mature bulbs, insures the best final results.

The reproductive strategies of some bulbs are so unusual they defy the expectations of many gardeners. Lilies and some other species develop miniature bulbs called bulbils, in the axis of their leaves. All along the stems, tucked into the spot where the leaf attaches to the plant, little knobs appear. By the end of the growing season they look like miniature versions of the parent plants. You may have noticed their presence on the edge of a clump of lilies in the garden. Tiny single-leaved lily plants pop out of the ground in the spring where they fell from last year's overhanging stems.

If I want to reproduce the plant I pick the bulbils off late in the season and store them over the winter in a bag of vermiculite in the vegetable crisper of the refrigerator. They can be planted in soil trays just below the surface in late winter or early spring.

Another way of increasing lilies, or for that matter other true bulbs with scales, like amaryllis, narcissus, lycoris, and nerine, is a technique called twin scaling. Think of the bulb as a cooking onion. To do twin scalings, trim off the roots up to the base plate. Next, cut off the upper third of the bulb horizontally. Then cut the bulbs vertically, leaving as much of the base plate attached to each segment as possible. The number of sections you can make depends on the size of the bulb. Small bulbs are best quartered, but you can cut larger bulbs into smaller sections as long as there is a piece of the base plate attached.

Fan the scales out in each section and cut through the base plate so that each little piece of base plate has two pieces of scale attached. Loosely place the scales in a plastic bag with slightly moistened vermiculite and a little fungicide, and no consideration for which way is up. Put the bag in a shaded spot at comfortable room temperature. An out of the way box under my desk has worked for me. It can take six to eight weeks for a tiny bulb to develop where the base plate joins the scales. It's important throughout to permit occasional air to enter so that the proto-bulb does not become infected with fungi that will quickly kill it. If you have been successful, there will be a tiny bulb with a few roots and withering scales that fed the developing bulb. Plant these with the bulb under the soil, leaving part of the scale above the surface. Some books recommend planting the scales themselves, without any preparation, but this method has worked better for me.

*T*ubers, such as begonia and gloxinia, can be divided when dormant by cutting them up before planting, a technique that will be familiar to anyone who has grown potatoes in a vegetable garden. Large tubers can show evidence of three or four shoots. Cut the tuber between the shoots, making sure the cut pieces are not too small and each holds at least one shoot.

Dust the cut sections with sulfur, powdered charcoal, or bulb dust to prevent fungal rot. Allow them to heal and dry a little in the open air for a day or so before planting. The best planting method is to half-bury the tuber in a pot, with just the buds showing above the surface of the soil. Then water the pot and place it in a warm, shaded place until the buds begin to unfurl. Water cautiously until the leaves take on bushy growth.

Tubers can also be reproduced from stem cuttings. This approach works well with begonias and gloxinias; it's also an excellent way to propagate dahlias. To get stem cuttings, tuck the tubers into the soil, without burying them completely, and water. I put newspaper over the containers to act like greenhouse protection. I then place the pots in a warm spot. New shoots should appear quickly in the warm, protected atmosphere; once they're visible, remove the newspapers. When the stems are about 4 inches tall, cut them off at the base. Dunk their ends in a hormone rooting powder or one of the liquid gel equivalents, and then place in a moist, soilless potting medium for a couple of weeks in a warm spot. Each stem cutting will develop its own roots and form a new plant and, eventually, a new bulb that will be an exact copy of the mother bulb. As an added bonus, I save a shoot or two on the original bulb and still get flowers from it that year.

To encourage rooting I use a plastic propagator with a high-domed, clear lid that permits air to enter and leave through holes. This helps to mitigate fungal buildup inside the propagator while maintaining conditions that are still moist enough to keep the leaves turgid. Once the cuttings have developed roots, they can be potted in separate containers or put right in the garden, in the case of dahlias. I get flowers the first season with this method.

Some bulbs can be started from leaf cuttings, a technique that is sometimes used to start begonias. Pieces of the leaf with the veins pointing downward are inserted into moist growing medium after a light dusting with root hormone. Bulbs have been grown

Seeds of the amaryllis
ready for planting out.

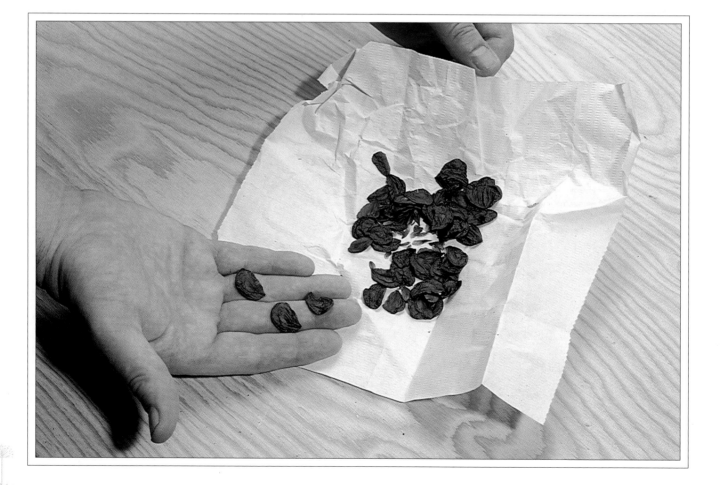

from whole leaves of the genus *Lachenalia* and *Scadoxus* treated this way, but I must confess that these are techniques for the die-hard experimenter who refuses to take the easy way out.

Propagation may sound like a complicated procedure considering the easy availability of tender bulbs. But the joys of propagation are both subtle and dramatic. Plants can be saved by taking cuttings or rescuing rotted bulbs. And whole ecosystems can benefit from being preserved by dedicated gardeners who propagate rare but unspectacular species.

*G*ROWING FROM SEED

Before I began growing tender bulbs with some zeal, I always thought of bulbs as, well, bulbs. The bulb itself was the beginning and the end of the exercise. I didn't really think of how they started, though I knew, of course, that bulbs, like almost all the plants we grow, begin as seeds. It was only after I tried to acquire some particularly hard-to-find species that I learned that the only way I could get them was as seed. Once I accepted this, I discovered that growing bulbs from seed was a lot easier than I had thought it would be.

The object of my desire was the South African bulb *Veltheimia bracteata*, the forest lily of Natal. It has aloelike pink and yellow flowers and undulating, shiny green leaves that make it very attractive. It's not particularly rare, and I had grown it as a bulb once before, but finding it locally a second time was proving difficult. A letter to the Indigenous Bulb

A tray of bulb seedlings in 4-inch pots about six months after planting.

Growers Association of South Africa brought a windfall of seeds. Not just veltheimias, but others I had never heard of. I've been growing bulbs from seed ever since, with more success than failure so far.

One of the difficulties of growing Southern Hemisphere bulbs in the Northern Hemisphere, and vice versa, is that imported bulbs arrive six months out of phase. When southern bulbs arrive here they may have been held too long in storage, often sprouted and withered and way past their prime. Success can be spotty unless they are pampered into life again. It's often not worthwhile.

Seeds are a way of coping with this difficulty. They can be started at the appropriate time to match the local growing season. They get into climatic phase immediately. You'll grow bulbs you never grew before by starting them from seed.

I sow half the seed when I receive it and save the rest for a later crop or a reseeding if my first one is a failure. But I am careful about how I store my seed. Many bulb seeds lose their vitality rapidly, their fleshy cases withering like prunes, especially if kept in an old tin box from year to year. I keep mine in the refrigerator in plastic prescription bottles or transparent film cans.

I plant the first half of the seeds in shallow, 4-inch green plastic pots filled with a finer version of my regular potting mix (see page 34). I dampen my starting medium below by standing the pots in water before sprinkling the soil with seeds. I spread them around, mindful of the year or more they will have to spend here growing larger. I cover the seeds with about a quarter inch of compost and then a light covering of silver sand to retard the growth of the algae, which likes to take hold in the moist conditions of a seed bed. The silver sand can also indi-cate when the pot needs watering, turning from a duller gray when moist to silver again when it is dry.

For a hard-to-start seed, especially if it is fine, I start it on a brick. I take an ordinary red house brick, without holes, and put it in an open plastic pan with water about halfway up the brick. I put about a quarter of an inch of fine seed-starting mix on the upper surface of the brick, making a nice flat planting area up to ½-inch thick. I sprinkle this with seed and leave it uncovered. Osmosis carries the water to the seeds, keeping them constantly moist, but surrounded by plenty of fresh air to prevent algae and fungus from growing in the medium. I get terrific germination with this technique on many small-seeded bulbs like gloxinia and begonia. When seedlings are large enough I prick them out with a knife blade and pot them in their own individual pots. I place the pots in a plastic propagator with a high-domed lid that is designed to let air in and out through a couple of holes. Once the lid is on, the propagator acts like a mini-greenhouse. I take the lid off once the plants have started to grow on and grow the sprouts for about a year in the same pot, keeping it moist as long as the seedlings remain green, and letting it dry out when their leaves have died down at the beginning of dormancy. In summer I put the seedlings in shade outdoors or behind a shade cloth in a window when the weather outside is too cold.

Some seeds can take a month or more to germinate, while others appear in just a few days. I've found that usually either germination is pretty high or the crop is a total failure. I am always asking myself questions about each experiment. Was I out of seasonal synch? Did I water enough? After failures I try reseeding later with the spare seeds I saved.

Veltheimia seedlings about eight months after planting, being potted up into individual cells in seedling packs. They'll stay in these for another eight months.
Here are the first Veltheimia seedlings 2½ years after planting.

I'VE FOUND that every time I try something new with seeds, or other forms of propagation, I end up with many more bulbs than I need, so beware. Once you start growing your own, you will find that tender bulbs are a large universe whose charms are still relatively untapped.

Summer Bulbs You Can Grow

GARDENERS HAVE NEVER HAD IT SO GOOD WHEN IT COMES TO variety. On my desk right now is the spring catalog of a well-known bulb company. By choosing something from every category of tender bulbs I could have the beginnings of a pretty fair tender bulb collection. What would I choose if I were starting such a collection today?

For my garden I would choose *Acidanthera murielae* for its tall and strikingly scented white, purple-blotched flowers and grow it with some species gladiolus and crocosmia. There would be some hybrid achimenes for their cozy brilliance in a shady pot. Tall trumpets of crinum flowers would bloom in late summer in pots, while in a shady spot caladiums could grow alongside tuberous begonias.

A pot of clivia gives scores of orange flowers in a shady summer location outdoors. Try the Ornithogalums, like saundersiae, in pots or in the garden. Oxalis makes an equally pretty garden edging and a pot plant, with many color varieties. In pots, nerines make excellent autumn-flowering plants. Tigridias are extremely unusual and quite easy for midsummer bloom in pots or right in the garden. Vallotas, or Scarborough lilies, have been cultivated successfully for hundreds of years for their wonderful red trumpet flowers. Try Sprekelia in pots for an appearance that makes me think of orchids.

After experience with these, I would try any of the species listed in the following pages. It may be the beginning of a beautiful friendship.

Achimenes

(a-KIM-inees)

From the South American tropics, this plant makes an interesting hanging-pot plant from bulbs that look like scaly pine cones. It is an easy starter bulb and very rewarding to grow. The plants have unusual hairy leaves and big open-faced tubular flowers in many colors. They need an early start indoors. I start mine right in the pots in a fluffy, soilless commercial planting mix in midwinter, planting half a dozen rhizomes in a shallow 6-inch pot about an inch deep and a few inches apart. I water once very well and then not at all until growth starts. I keep the plants in a warm, moist, shady place in at least 65°F until growth starts. They should begin to flower in late spring and continue throughout the summer. Keep the pot evenly moist without waterlogging it.

In autumn, when flowering ends, bring the pot indoors and store dry at 50° to 60°F. Growth will begin again in early spring, when you should resume watering. Replant in new soil every couple of years. To avoid disturbing the roots I do this in midwinter when the bulbs are completely dormant so that the new roots can immediately plunge into good soil. Plenty of colorful hybrids are available, from white through reds, purples, blues, and rare yellows.

Acidanthera

(ass-id-AN-the-rah)

Now included in gladiolus by some authorities, *Acidanthera murielae* is one of my favorite outdoor summer-garden bulbs. Native to the highlands of Ethiopia, this gladiolus-like white flower with the purple stain in the throat has it all: fragrance, late-

Achimines 'Desiree'. The tiny pine cone–like rhizomes have been bred to produce flowers in colors from crimson through lavender blues to white, that bloom much of the summer and beyond.

or so in sunshine store the bulbs in perlite or brown paper bags at about 60°F until it is time to plant again. If I've left them in their pots in a warm, dry place over the winter, I shake out the bulbs, trim off the old worn-out corms at the base of the new ones, and put the new top corm into fresh soil to begin the cycle once again. Grow cormels into full-size plants by planting them in a small separate pot to grow for a summer.

Agapanthus

Nile lily

Agapanthus africans from South Africa has no true bulbs, but fleshy rhizomes put it in the bulb camp. With clustered heads of alliumlike bluish purple to white flowers, aga-panthus is usually planted in pots unless grown in a frost-free zone. There are both deciduous and ever-green species, although I have never seen the decid-uous species available in North America. You're like-liest to find *A. minimus* (a miniature version available as Peter Pan) and *A. africanus*, the regular-sized one. Both come in either blue- or white-flow-ered varieties. The plants bloom well in containers, and this is the best way to grow them in colder cli-mates, although all are half-hardy. Avoid dividing because it hampers flowering for a year or two, but if you must, divide by splitting the plants in spring. Plant in rich soil. Keep watered at all times, except

summer bloom, and good looks because rain does not spot the flowers. Flowering is continuous with up to ten blooms appearing over a period of about a month. The only drawback is that it hates starting out in cool weather. I never plant outdoors until June, and then I think twice. Sometimes it won't even bloom in cooler climates. The answer is to plant early (March) in pots and put the plants out only in warm weather. At that point, I take the root ball out of the pot and put it gently into a pre-prepared hole in the garden. Plant in well-drained soil (50-50 soil-less mix and sand in pots) in a sunny spot about 4 inches deep. Lift plants before frost and after a day

Agapanthus. A great container plant for blue or white summer blooms on the patio.

(Opposite): Alstroemeria 'Yellow King'. These need cool, moist conditions for best flowers.

Albuca canadensis, named because it was mistakenly classified as coming from Canada, not South Africa, its true home.

in winter, when it should be somewhat drier. Grow in full sun. Even out of bloom the strap-shaped leaves provide a nice cascade of green.

Albuca

(al-BEU-kah)

Albuca canadensis, with pale yellow-green flowers with green stripes, is the best known of the 11 species of this South African genus. The plant's name proves that even a genius like Linnaeus can be wrong. He named it because it was listed in a book about Canadian native plants, and the misleading name has stuck ever since. Alas, none of the members of this genus can overwinter outdoors anywhere near Canada. All are tender. When grown outdoors as garden subjects, as they often are, the bulbs should be planted after the last frost in a humus-rich sandy soil if possible. Flowers will appear in late spring or early summer. Dig up and store dry at about 50°F over winter before replanting again in the spring. The bulbs reproduce willingly from offsets or seed.

Alstroemeria

(al-stre-MEE-ree-ah)

Peruvian lily

Alstroemerias are native to South America and grow from brittle, fleshy white rhizomes. There are about ten species and many hybrids, all of which are half-hardy. The flowers resemble azaleas and are often streaked and spotted with darker colors on yellow or orange bases. There are two ways to treat these plants. Where it is warm enough outdoors, anywhere south of Maryland, the secret to success is to not lift them in autumn like other tender bulbs. Plant at least 6 inches deep in rich soil and do not disturb. Planted in pots, alstroemerias can simply be taken indoors and kept dry in winter, to be restarted again in March. Don't expect a good show of flowers in the first year, and try to avoid dividing as long as possi-

ble for best results. But once they get going, look out. Best in full sun or slight shade.

Amaryllis

Belladonna lily, naked ladies

Amaryllis from South Africa is the only true amaryllis and should not be confused with hippeastrum, the pot-bellied bulb that goes under the common name amaryllis and is sold virtually everywhere in late autumn. The true amaryllis's common names come from the sudden appearance of the tall flower stalks without any leaves. Just as quickly, the flower bud opens to reveal eight to twelve pale pink, heavily scented trumpet-shaped flowers. The strap-shaped leaves do not appear until flowering is over. Amaryllis is half-hardy and can be grown outdoors if planted 6 to 8 inches deep in midsummer. When planted in pots, the top third of the bulb can remain above the surface. Once planted, it should not be disturbed unless absolutely necessary or it may not flower — sometimes for years. In fact, benign ne-

glect is probably the best way to treat this, not watering at all when the flower dies down, and then only slightly in late summer to encourage the naked ladies.

Once planted, a newly bought bulb should flower right away. When the flowers have faded, encourage the leaf growth in a cool, bright area until early spring, then dry out the bulb completely by simply putting it in a cool, dark closet until all growth ceases and the bulb goes dormant. Keep it that way with no moisture at all until it's time to plant again in July.

Amaryllis has been crossed with several other large bulbs, including brunsvigia, crinum, and nerine to produce amarcrimun, amnerine and brunsdonna. My amarcrinum blooms for me in early summer and often again in September. Try any of the hybrids if you can find them in the catalogs.

Outdoors, plant in full sun in well-drained soil or the usual 50-50 mix of soilless mix and sand. Propagation is from old bulb offsets or seed, although the seed can take five or six years to flower.

(Opposite left): Anomatheca laxa, also called Lapeirousia cruenta. These bulbs will bloom from seed in a year.

(Opposite right): Arisaema candidissimum is the Chinese version of our North American Jack-in-the-Pulpit.

Amaryllis belladonna. The famous naked ladies, so named because the flowers come and go before the foliage has fully arrived.

Anomatheca

(a-NOH-ma-thee-ka)

Anomatheca is a South African genus with about six species that used to be listed under *Lapeirousia*, but now have a taxonomic home of their own. The likeliest to be found is sold as *A. laxa* or *A. cruenta* and is carmine red with a darker red blotch on some of the petals. There are also white and blue forms with similar darker spots. These bulbs make excellent pot plants. In southern California they bloom happily in rockeries, growing to a height of 8 to 12 inches in summer. Elsewhere, they may be grown in pots where they bloom from February on. In warmer climates, the irregular bulbs can be planted outdoors in March just under the surface. When grown in pots, plant ten or so of the corms just under the surface of a 50-50 mix of sand and potting mix in early au-

tumn and keep them as cool as possible, short of freezing. Start them up by watering sparingly until the leaves emerge, then place in a cool, bright room (and I mean cool, not the living room) until the spike appears. They should begin flowering by early spring. Propagation is from seeds and cormels.

Arisaema

(a-ris-EYE-mah)

Arisaema come mostly from Asia, but the group includes the common Jack-in-the-pulpit of North American woods. Their best points are their bizarre flowers and sometimes striped and veined leaves. They are fashionable as garden subjects in the cool, moist climate of England. Here, *A. candidissimum* is the likeliest to be encountered, with its white hood-like spathe, sometimes veined with pink and green.

Aristea major grows 4 feet high and carries ephemeral flowers in shades of blue.

All species need boglike conditions, and the tropicals prefer plenty of warmth. Reduce watering in winter, but never let these plants dry completely.

Aristea

(a-ris-TEE-ah)
Aristea is an irislike plant from South Africa that prefers wetter conditions than most of the bulbs on this list. It's an example of the kind of bulb to try when you've grown bored with ordinary bulbs. Seeds are available and are probably the easiest way to achieve success with this rhizomatous plant. The tall plants have irislike leaves and ephemeral flowers in shades of blue, making them excellent companion plants to other tall bulbs, like watsonia. The rhizomes should be planted in rich soil in full sun or partial shade in autumn or spring. Give them plenty of water during the growing season, then dry out over winter in their pots. *A. major* is probably the best of the species and the likeliest available from seed catalogs. Plant seed in two batches: as soon as received and again in spring, or about six months apart to assure germination. They should flower in three years from seedlings.

Babiana

(bab-ee-AH-nah)
There are about 30 species of this South African corm, which got its name from the fondness baboons have for eating them. They are related to gladiolus, but have smaller, one-inch flowers that run about 10 to 20 per stem, like small freesias. The leaves are

pleated, ribbed, and hairy, making them easy to identify. Most bulbs available are hybrids with numerous color combinations of blue, purple, and white. The best species are *B. plicata*, an ultramarine blue with white center, and *B. rubrocyanea*, which is dark blue and red-throated.

These can be grown in well-drained soil in the rock garden, where they are planted after the last frost for summer flowers. They can also be grown in pots to follow their natural cycle: planted up to 6 inches deep in a favorite mix in autumn and kept in a cool, bright room or greenhouse where they will bloom in late spring. Dry out after flowering and store in dry peat or perlite or in their pots until time to restart the cycle again.

Begonia

(be-GOH-nee-ah)

Of the hundreds of species of this genus from warm regions all over the world, only the tuberous begonias of South America interest growers of tender bulbs. The tubers should be planted in February, hollow side up, with their upper surface above the soil, in rich, organic soil and kept at 60° to 70°F until leafy shoots appear. Allow them to leaf out indoors until the first summer weather permits placing them outdoors. Water and feed regularly with a balanced fertilizer all summer, and remember they grow best all summer in cool semishade, sheltered from wind, which reduces flowering. Stop watering at the first sign of frost and lift the entire plant, including all foliage and roots, and store in a warm, dry place. Once the leaves have withered, cut them off and store the tubers in the coolest part of the house, so long as it never goes below 35°F. I use an unoccupied room in the main house. Potted begonias are best just stored, foliage and all, until spring, when they should be removed and put into new soil. Propagate from seeds or divided tubers that have at least one growing point showing on the surface. Dust the cut edges with sulfur or charcoal dust and plant when a slight callus forms.

(Top): Babiana stricta. The early Dutch settlers named these for the baboons that found the bulbs so tasty.

(Bottom): Begonia 'Sceptre' is one of the hundreds of striking hybrids grown in baskets by thousands of gardeners each summer.

Bessera.

Bessera

(BES-a-rah)

Bessera elegans is a member of the Lily family from Mexico. The fingernail-sized bulbs produce three or four long thin leaves that spread out on the ground and are followed by a wiry stem up to 20 inches long that ends with about a dozen tiny fuchsialike flowers. There are three brick red outer segments, and three inner segments of red with a white stripe and long violet stamens that protrude beyond the ends of the flower, giving the effect of a fuchsia. These half-hardy bulbs are very arresting when planted in a mass. To achieve this effect, bury half a dozen of the bulbs an inch or so deep in a pot in early spring.

They can also be planted outdoors in early summer. Small but arresting flowers appear from June to September, depending on when they were planted. Lift bulbs in autumn and store in peat at 50°F, or leave them to dry in their pots at no less than 50°F until time to restart them again.

Cannas are a favorite outdoor summer plant. They are not strictly bulbs, but fleshy rhizomes, and because they are cultivated in a similar way, they are included among tender bulbs.

Canna

Beloved of municipal decorating schemes, these relatives of the banana from the tropical regions of the world are among our oldest decorative garden plants. Cannas are recorded as growing at Padua, Italy, in 1579. I put a few in a big clay pot on my front porch every summer and they are a constant delight, in bloom with large carmine flowers from midsummer until frost. There are at least 50 species, but I mostly grow hybrids that now come with flowers of red, pink, purple, yellow, and orange combined with large decorative leaves in shades of green, bronze, and purple and variegated. I start the rhizomes in a soilless mix in March, watering sparingly at first and increasing it as the foliage grows. Once roots have started I put two or three clumps in a large pot and transfer them outdoors in early June or plant them directly into the garden where they must be kept moist at all times for best results. New rhizomes throw up shoots that flower throughout the summer. Cannas come in both tall and dwarf varieties. When frost hits I lift the plants and dry them before cutting off most of the stem and storing in a warm, dry place over the winter. Rhizomes can be cut between growing points and repotted once they have started into growth.

Chasmanthe floribunda,
a vigorous grower that
likes a wet area, but
adapts almost anywhere
it likes the climate.

*(Opposite): Chlidanthus
fragrans* blooms in a
neglected corner of a
garden.

Chasmanthe

(chaz-MANTH-ee)

Chasmanthe is a Cape bulb that naturalizes freely in warm climates. There are three species that have long-tubed flowers in colors from yellow through orange to red. Chasmanthe will also grow in large pots and blooms best when undisturbed. Its needs are few and it is one of the easiest plants to start from seed. The only limiting factor is cold weather. Plant the corms in spring in pots of a bulb mix. Move outdoors in summer, with plenty of water, and then take the pots indoors to a cool greenhouse or bright, cool room to overwinter. They rapidly grow up to 3 feet tall as early as the second season when kept in sun or partial shade and can become either a pest or an important garden subject depending on your growing skills and point of view.

Chlidanthus

(klid-ANTH-us)

Chlidanthus fragrans, or perfumed fairy lily, has four or more pretty, star-shaped bright yellow flowers. They come from the Andes. They are usually offered in spring catalogs and should be potted up in early spring, a half dozen to a pot. Once the weather warms up I put them, pot and all, into the garden so the pot rim is at ground level. They should flower by midsummer, and you should encourage leaves to grow by applying plenty of balanced fertilizer. Bring them in before the first frost and keep dry over the winter. Repot the bulbs in fresh soil in the spring. In the southern United States, the sun-loving chlidanthus is often grown in gardens where it thrives year-round. Elsewhere, chlidanthus looks best crowded in pots. Plant the bulbs near the surface so that the spare foliage can make a nice display.

Clivia miniata,
or Kaffir lily.

(Opposite): Crinum moorei 'Alba'. The white form of this favorite pot plant.

Clivia

(CLIVE-ee-ah)
Clivia miniata is an excellent beginner's plant and one I grow all year with great satisfaction, even when it is not in flower. The *miniata* part of this South African native is a real misnomer. It doesn't mean small. Plants can easily grow to become 3 feet in diameter. I had to take an ax to mine when I finally divided it out of a 20-inch pot. Actually the *miniata* comes from *minium,* Latin for "red oxide of lead," which describes the color of the flowers, not the size of the plant, which with offshoots can have 60 or more tube-shaped flowers over a month in midsummer. They will also bloom again in the winter if kept in a cool greenhouse. But clivia makes a fabulous year-round houseplant as well. The shiny green thick straps of leaves look vaguely Victorian and continue to look great all winter.

A new plant of clivia usually arrives as a couple of leaves attached to some thick white roots. Plant in a pot appropriate to the eventual size of the plant, at least 8 inches in diameter, in a rich potting mix. I

grow clivia in a commercial black plastic pot with a little give because clivia roots can be so vigorous they easily shatter clay pots. I simply pot the ever-growing plant in successively larger containers until I can't move the pots anymore. Keep in semishade during the summer and water regularly. For best flowers, feed occasionally with a balanced fertilizer, without overfeeding. In winter reduce water. I keep mine in the bedroom during winter to give the room a much-needed touch of green when snows are blowing. In spring, I just put the pot outdoors and increase watering. Flowers soon follow.

Crinum

(CRY-num)

There are about 130 crinum species around the world, but only one or two are generally available for cultivation. I consider this a "must-have" bulb for anyone starting out. I plant the large bulb in a pot in late spring, with the top third of the bulb above the surface, and water sparingly until growth begins. Then I give plenty of water throughout the summer until a tall stem with about ten rose pink trumpet-shaped flowers appears. It doesn't even seem to mind if I don't dry it out completely in winter. I grow mine in pots because crinum hates being disturbed. When autumn comes I take the pots in and try to ignore the ratty look of the long leaves, which die from the ends back. I reduce or even cease watering in the winter. I rest the bulbs in their pots in a cool room, restarting the bulbs in a sunny window in March. Every few years I move my plants to a pot a couple of inches larger without disturbing the soil. I lift the clump and its root ball out of the old pot in spring, when the bulb is actively growing, and fill in around it with fresh mix. Then I water and wait.

Crocosmia

(kro-KOS-mee-ah)

I envy all gardeners with half-hardy conditions who can grow these South African bulbs outdoors all year long. A friend grows his on a windy southern Welsh hillside against stone walls with no problems. They take on gigantic proportions, with long sword-shaped leaves and great zigzags of blooms, particularly the huge scarlet cultivar 'Lucifer'. But crocosmia can be grown, less prodigiously, as pot plants, too, for a summer patio, as I do. They are also sold under the name montbretia. They look good in a herbaceous border where they blend well with perennials. Colors range from very tender yellows to hardier scarlets, with orange-reds in between. I lift mine at the end of the summer and store them in brown paper bags after they have dried for a week or two. I replant them outdoors in May for blooms by August. I plant 3 inches deep in rich, sandy soil for best flowers.

Cypella

(seye-PEL-ah)

This unusual irislike plant from Central and South America emerges from scaly, elongated corms and is grown in gardens as a background or filler plant in sunny borders. Closely related to tigridias, the flowers look like Siberian irises but are mostly in the yellow, orange, and white range of colors. The flowers blossom in the morning to fade by nightfall, but blossoms are produced continuously over a long period, sometimes from spring to fall. They bloom best in a hot, sunny location. *C. herbertii* is the most commonly grown species, and one of the easiest. Start the plant in spring in a well-drained, sandy soil, but keep it very warm and in bright light to bloom. They can be started from seeds or clumps, and when cooler weather comes they should be stored dry indoors in pots or loose bundles to be restarted when warm weather returns.

Cyrtanthus

(kur-TANTH-us)

Cyrtanthus is the new name for *Vallota speciosa* (now called *C. elatus*) and is still often sold under the old name. There are a number of species, which have starlike to tubular flowers up to 3 inches across and come in red, white, pink, orange, and yellow. All are best grown as pot plants.

To start, take a few bulbs and plant them in a 50-50 blend of soilless mix and sand in midsummer and water cautiously until roots develop. Flowers will appear at the end of summer, followed by strap-shaped leaves. Continue watering until the leaves die, by early spring; then stop watering completely until it is time to restart the bulbs again in midsummer. Scarborough lilies, as they are also called, are excellent indoor houseplants if they can be kept slightly cooler (50°F) during their resting period. Do not repot if you can help it, and your bulbs will grow better.

(Opposite, top left): Crocosmia 'Lucifer'. I would try these in a sheltered spot if I lived south of New York.

(Opposite, bottom): Cypella herbertii. Not as showy as some, cypella is a great background plant in a rock garden.

(Opposite, top right): Cyrtanthus mackenii. Grow these in pots like their close relatives, the crinums.

Dahlia

These tuberous-rooted summer bloomers grow wild in Mexico and Guatemala. There are few flowers that have bent to man's hand as effectively as the dahlia. Over the years they have been bred into a variety of rigid forms to satisfy the needs of salon gardeners with dominance complexes, losing much of their original charm in the process. That said, I still grow them for their huge lush strands of color in late summer and the perky impudence of the smaller kinds in a summer border.

A number of catalogs list named varieties, but pictures can be deceiving, and I've often been disappointed in what came up. Seeing an actual specimen in a garden is another matter. I have shamelessly knocked on doors and begged tubers from the surprised occupants.

Tubers are sold beginning in early spring, usually as a bulb with a green bud at the top. As soon as I receive them, I put one tuber in a 6-inch pot of soilless mixture, like Pro-Mix, with the green bud above the surface, which should be about halfway down the pot. This is so that I can add soil when the bud begins to grow into a stem. I water the tuber thoroughly and put it in a warm, humid place with a page from the newspaper placed loosely over the pot.

Dahlias need a warm environment, so I time my pregrowing in pots up to a month before I can count on 70°F weather outdoors, or when the lilacs stop blooming. Then I put a shovelful of compost and a handful of pelleted bonemeal at the bottom of my planting hole before sliding the root ball out and burying the plant, without disturbing the roots, to the level it was in the pot. I put a tall stake in the ground at the same time. Dahlias give the garden a wonderful lift at a season when few perennials of any consequence are in rampant bloom.

Plant in full sun or part shade. Planting the tubers directly into the ground will give later flowers,

Dahlia hybrid.

Dierama pendulum growing in front of a bed of *Kniphofia*, another crossover species often included among the bulbs.

and in my climate we get only one or two blooms before frost comes and blackens the foliage. For the largest flowers, remove all but the terminal bud when they appear. Keep soil around the plants moist during the entire growth period. Mulching with compost is a big help.

Dig them up after frost has killed the top growth. There will be a number of tubers hanging from the main stem. Shake off the dirt, cut the stem to 4 or 5 inches, and store in a paper bag with their label or wrapped in newspapers at 35° to 45°F. Don't divide the tubers until the spring, when you are ready to plant. It's easier to see the new growing points then. Just cut down the stem to include a tuber with a new growing point, and plant so the growing point is at the soil surface.

Many gardeners have tired of the rigid system of shapes and flower forms and are going back to growing the species, like *D. imperialis*. These are still hard to find but easy to grow. Growing the dwarf dahlias for pots or low borders in the garden is best done from seed, and the seed is readily available in garden centers. A planting by February gives me blooms by July.

Dierama

(dy-e-RAH-mah)

This South African genus of about 25 species is a bulb that likes moist conditions. *D. pulcherrimum* and *D. pendulum*, its smaller relative, are the most commonly grown species, and both can be considered half-hardy. Garden designers like to put the bulbs at the edge of a pool so that the arching pink bells can live up to their common name, angel's fishing rod. Plant the corms 2 inches deep and allow to spread if they can be left outside, which they can, as far north as Virginia. In colder climes grow them in pots that can be sunk into the ground in summer and taken indoors for a dry rest during the winter months. Restart the bulbs by watering the soil when the weather warms up. Seeds will flower in two to three years and will spread like weeds where they like the conditions.

Eucharis

(EU-kah-ris)
Eucharis is from South America, and the species *E. grandiflora* is the most commonly available. Mine produces wonderfully shiny green leaves, like fat spear points, that make the plant attractive even when it is not in bloom. Moist warmth is the secret to growing this bulb. The trouble is, it's hard to

bloom this eucharis unless conditions are right. With the proper treatment, however, plants can be induced to flower several times a year. You must dry the compost for a few months before starting to water again. Grow in a greenhouse or under artificial lights at 65°–75°F. The bulbs are best obtained in the winter, when they should be planted immediately in loose, well-drained, fibrous soil. Flowers appear almost immediately after the bulbs are planted. I grow mine outdoors in semishade over the summer, with plenty of water and fertilizer. In autumn, I reduce watering without allowing the leaves to die. Eucharis bloom in winter. After blooming, I gradually restart the watering schedule, increasing watering as the days grow warmer. Because this bulb dislikes disturbance, I don't try to divide the bulbs as they fill the pot. This results in no flowers. I just lift the root ball out of the pot and put it into a pot a couple of inches wider in circumference. I drop at least a couple of inches of fresh soil in the bottom, firm, and put in the root ball and fill in with more fresh soil around the sides.

Eucomis

(you-KOM-is)
This South African native is one of the least troublesome bulbs I've ever encountered. This excellent pot plant includes about ten species and

(Opposite): Eucomis autumnalis. The pineapple lily of southern Africa is easy to grow and rebloom year after year.

Eucharis grandiflora, the tropical daffodil, comes from the eastern slopes of the Andes, in Colombia.

Ferraria crispa likes a moist location to bloom the flowers that are often compared to Odontoglossum orchids.

blooms for me for most of the summer. I grow three varieties, including *E. comosa*, *E. autumnalis* 'White Dwarf', and an unnamed pink variety. All produce a striking rosette of wavy leaves, sometimes spotted with burgundy, and a flower spike reminiscent of a pineapple that gives them their common name, pineapple lily. The flowers range from white through yellow-green to pink. In milder and more tropical areas eucomis can be grown as garden plants year-round. Once they begin to bloom in midsummer, they seem to go on for months and display well as pot plants. When the leaves go limp in the autumn rains, I take the pots inside and store them dry in a dark place above 50°F. Once the weather warms up in spring, I simply top-dress with fresh soil and start watering the pots. They easily produce offsets that can be broken off and potted up separately in rich

soil in the spring when watering begins. They can also be propagated by seeds that bloom in about four years.

Ferraria

(fe-RAY-ree-ah)

These South African members of the Iris family have been cultivated in Europe since 1755, but they are still rare through no fault of their own. Their unusual color combinations of spotted flowers with frilly petals are fascinating, but they last only a few days. They have what has sometimes been described as a strong scent, but pollinators seem to like them. Outdoors, you can plant these small bulbs up to 6 inches deep in equal proportions of potting mix, sand, and pea gravel and place them in a sunny but

Freesias are grown for the variety of colors and heady fragrance during their winter blooming.

moist position, with a dryer period in the winter. If you grow them in pots, start the bulbs in autumn and grow cool over the winter in a greenhouse or bright, cool room. Put the pots outdoors in semishade to bloom in the summer. In autumn bring the pots indoors to remain cool and dry over the winter until they can be started outdoors again in spring, the pots top-dressed with fresh compost.

Freesia

(FREE-zhah)

In the wild, this South African species looks little like the highly selected hybrids grown today as multihued, wonderfully scented cut flowers. I grow *F. elimensis,* a white species with a yellow lip spot and purplish undersides on the petals. The pointed corms

are available from garden centers. Some sellers have them in precooled condition available in the spring so that they can be planted to bloom almost immediately. Plant the corms six to a 6-inch pot at least 4 inches down to hold up the heavy stem of tubular flowers. They make a striking late-winter show in a window, particularly when grown cool, wet, and bright. Flowering will occur from midwinter to as late as early summer depending on when you start the corms. When the leaves die down, store the corms dry in peat. I caution, however, that if they have not been grown or stored cool enough, they will not bloom again. For best results, restart the corms in summer in a cool, shady place and bring the pots indoors in autumn to grow cool over the winter. Freesias grow quite happily in a commercial soilless mix.

Galtonia

(gaul-TOH-nee-ah)

Galtonia is a South African bulb that is an excellent choice for planting right in the garden. *G. candicans* are commonly available and grow about 3 feet high, with hanging, bell-like blooms. The effect is like a giant hyacinth. They look great bunched together in a herbaceous border. In warmer climates with well-drained soil they can remain in the ground year-round. Plant 6 inches deep in rich soil. In my area I lift them and store them dry over the winter, then restart in a pot in March. In May I unpot them and transfer to the garden. In warmer climates, south of Maryland, they can be planted in the autumn.

Galtonia candicans. In my garden, this one blooms in midsummer among the perennials.

Gladiolus

Gladiolus are the tulips of the tender bulb world: everyone grows them at one time or another. Some, like *G. Byzantium*, can be left outdoors year-round as far north as Zone 4. Hundreds of more tender hybrids are available, and they've been the mainstay of the cut-flower industry for years. So much so, that many gardeners are bored with them. But species gladiolus are an amazing world of their own. There are more than a hundred in Africa alone, with more being discovered regularly. Many bulb growers have made a lifetime hobby of just this genus. Certain hybrids have wintered in my yard, in Toronto, but glads work best as summer bloomers outdoors. The hybrids are divided into three groups: the early-flowering Nanus type, hybrids of the miniatures, and large-flowered hybrids. The Nanus group can be planted in autumn in a cool, bright area and will bloom in spring if you live up to Zone 4, or they can be planted in early summer to bloom in the autumn. Many garden centers carry these bulbs. They often also carry the colorful hybrids of the miniatures, with shorter stature and smaller flowers, or the large-flowered hybrids that can grow 5 feet high and carry flowers 4 or more inches wide. Both of these are also

Gladiolus cultivars growing among summer perennials.

Gloriosa rothschildiana is easy to bloom in pots on the summer porch with a cool rest in winter.

usually planted in a rich compost by April or May, about 4 inches or even deeper so that when the spike appears the whole plant does not topple over.

Gladiolus flowers can be either ephemeral or long-lasting depending on the species. Seeds are the best way to try some of the unusual species. Flowering from seed can take a few years. Glads can also reproduce from cormels. I think life is too short to grow just gladiolus, but a few in any collection are inevitably popular.

Gloriosa

(gloh-ree-OH-sah)

There are a number of named varieties of Gloriosa lily, like superba or rothschildiana, but most should only be considered superior examples of one climbing species that hangs onto nearby objects with its leaf tendrils. I once saw it covering trash heaps elegantly in a Balinese village. The plant is believed to have originated in Africa and India where different color variations developed. All are worth having and the plant is easy to grow from a tuber which is planted horizontally. I plant indoors in early spring in a pot of soilless mix to get a good month or two head start on the growing season. Then I take the plant out of its pot and plant the soil ball in a prepared hole in the ground with some bone meal and a light, composted soil. I give plenty of water during the entire growing season. If planted outdoors in full sun, the tuber should be placed near a shrub or trellis so that the wiry stems can wind their way around the support to give a lovely display when the flowers begin to open in the late summer. Tubers should be dug up and stored dry when the first frost hits. If grown in a pot, the tubers can be dried out for a month or so after flowering and then restarted for another blooming in the greenhouse or a moist and warm, bright room. I store my tubers dry in the pot over the winter and restart in new potting soil in the spring.

Haemanthus coccineus.

pot with a couple of inches of space between the bulb and the pot wall. When starting the bulb the first time, follow the usual procedure of watering well once and then sparingly to encourage root growth. These plants resent disturbance so they should be planted for a long stay. Water actively in the growing season when leaves are flourishing. They will bloom in midsummer. After blooming, the leaves will die back, and that's when to put the pot away to dry for a few months before restarting. Usually, the leaves appear only when the flowers are over. They live up to their name, creating a pincushion of blood red flowers with long protruding stamens on a 3-foot stalk. The effect from a distance is of a fireworks starburst. They are best grown as pot plants. Those who want to explore the more unusual flowers of this genus might try *H. albiflos*, or paint brush. It is a striking evergreen species that has white flowers with white bracts, all tipped with bright yellow anthers. The leaves have an oddly attractive fleshiness, as do many members of this family.

H. coccineus has been cultivated since 1605 but, strangely, like many of the attractive and easy-to-grow tender bulbs, is hard to find today. In their native habitat, these flowers bloom in late autumn, with the bulbs maturing during winter and into spring. They should be kept completely dry all sum-

Haemanthus

(heye-MANTH-us)

Some members of this genus have been placed in *Scadoxus* by some authorities because they have rhizomes. Call it what you may, this is a strikingly varied genus of about 60 South and Central African bulbs, the best known of which is the blood lily, formerly called *H. katherinae*. It's now known as *H. multiflorus* ssp. It is also considered almost as easy to grow as hippeastrum, the Christmas amaryllis. *H. multiflorus* is planted just under the soil surface in a 50-50 mix of sand and bagged growing medium in a

mer, before being started again in the autumn. Propagation of haemanthus is by offsets, leaf cuttings, and seeds, which should be removed from the pulp of the seed head and planted immediately just below the surface. With luck, they will bloom by the fourth year.

Hedychium

(hay-DI-kee-um)

The ginger lilies are from India and like their cousins, the cannas, enjoy moist, rich conditions from full sun to shade. I grow mine in big pots. *H. gardnerianum* has yellow flowers with red filaments. *H. coronarium* grows 3 feet tall and has white flowers. Other forms worth looking for include *H. flavescens* (orange) and *H. coccineum* (red, pink, or orange). I often grow these in straight soilless compost and place the pot in the shady part of my garden, where large-leaved plants shade the container. The base of the rhizomes remains shaded and moist while the upper leaves get as much sun as they can. They can also be planted right out in the garden for the summer. But I prefer to start them inside in pots in early spring so that a good root ball takes hold by the time I place the plants in the ground outdoors once the hot weather arrives. Plenty of water is the key to good growth once the bamboolike cane emerges from the ground. Blooms come in late summer, into autumn, depending on the species, and lend a tropical air to the rest of the garden. When the plant outgrows its home, I just repot, filling in around the root ball with new soil.

Hedychium coccineum,
the cultivar 'Honduras'.

Hippeastrum. The miniature hybrid 'Giraffe' grows 12–15 inches tall.

Hippeastrum

(hip-ee-AS-trum)

This is probably the most popular tender bulb, hippeastrum being the official name for the "amaryllis" that appears in groceries all over the country in the autumn for lush Christmas blooms. These days they come in shades from white to red and yellow and can be had in single blooms 8 inches across or in fantastic layered double forms. Trouble is, it would be charitable to say that one in a hundred of the bulbs ever blooms again. Follow these instructions exactly to make them bloom next year. For Christmas blooms, plant in September–October in a pot slightly larger than the bulb with the bulb about halfway down in the compost. Water thoroughly and gently apply bottom heat by keeping the pots in a place that is constantly warm, like on a steam heater or in a warm closet. Water again only when the soil seems dry. The bulbs will take eight weeks to bloom. After bloom, continue watering and feeding in the pot, and when warm weather arrives, take the bulb out of its pot and place it in rich garden soil to continue growing until late summer. By the first frost, dig the bulb up and lay it out on newspapers in a warm, dark place until the foliage dies down. Then cut the foliage off at the top of the bulb. Keep the bulb in a warm place until ready to start again, usually after a couple of months. Any offsets can be grown on continuously in a pot, without a dormant period, until they get to a mature size (about 2½ inches in diameter) when they are put on the adult regime as above.

Homeria ochroleuca.

Homeria

In its native habitat in South Africa, these brightly colored little bulbs can become weedy pests. In North America they are best grown in pots, except in some of the warmest areas. The flowers are star-shaped and come in varieties from orange through salmon to yellow. For those of us with perfect conditions and the right climate, homeria's adaptability and tenaciousness make it a good bulb for the rock garden all year long, and it is often available in early spring at garden centers for just this purpose. Plant 3 inches deep and a couple of inches apart in autumn, when they bloom in their native land. Grow on over winter with plenty of water, and dry out in spring, keeping the bulbs dormant over summer before restarting in autumn. Or dry them over the winter like glads after the first frost has killed the foliage.

Homoglossum watsonium.

Homoglossum

(homo-GLOSS-um)

This South African genus is often included with gladiolus and has been hybridized with it. Homoglossum flowers tend toward shades of red, with yellow throats. There are two ways to grow them. When the corms are planted in late spring, they produce flowers by late summer to early winter. They can be dried out and replanted again when warm weather returns. If planted in autumn in a sufficiently warm area, they will follow their natural cycle as winter growers, to be dried out and kept perfectly dry during the summer and then planted again or restarted in their pots. Here in the North, I treat them as I would gladiolus, planting outdoors in late spring.

Hymenocallis

(hy-men-oh-KAL-is)

Sometimes called spider lily, or Ismene, hymenocallis occurs naturally from the southern United States to the Andes. Most varieties have white flowers, with long recurved segments that give them a two-tiered look. There is also a yellow form called sulphur queen.

The baseball-sized bulbs are planted at least 6 inches deep in good, rich soil, and the first flowers bloom a month after planting. The flowers last longest when the plant is kept in a cool greenhouse, although the lack of one does not prevent an abundant show of fragrant, unusual flowers.

I have grown various forms of this bulb for years, and I love it, except for the fact that the stem grows too high, making it impossible to keep in a small pot. The plant invariably tips over, pot and all. Some gardeners put the bulbs in the ground for the summer in dappled shade where the strap-shaped leaves make interesting landscape subjects. It's a favorite of south Florida landscapers. Hymenocallis should be lifted before the first frost and stored dry and warm in the winter (above 50°F) either in their pots or in bags of powdered peat. Offsets form quickly and are the easiest way to increase your supply.

Ipheion

(i-FAY-on)

Ipheion, or spring star flower (*I. uniflorum*), is a South American species from the cool Andes that is often available in catalogs under the name brodiaea, triteleia, or milla. This is a half-hardy bulb with violet-blue star-shaped flowers that bloom in April if grown outdoors where the climate is warm enough. Potted bulbs will bloom almost immediately after they are started. Store completely dry when foliage

Ipheion uniflorum.

(Opposite): Hymenocallis 'Sulphur Queen'.

dies down. Restart in early spring. Superior color forms have been collected and are available. Divide clumps in autumn and replant immediately in their new site in a sheltered position in sun or light shade.

Ixia

(IX-iah)

Ixia is another South African corm that grows well in a rockery and is often available in the spring as a summer bulb in garden centers. There are about 50 species. In their native land, they are winter-growing and demand complete dryness in the summer. Flowers are star-shaped and colorful, with up to a dozen of them blooming on each stem in spring or summer. They are easily recognized by their dark red or brown centers with colors ranging from red through the oranges to white, yellow, and even green in the species *I. viridiflora*. They can be grown outdoors in a sheltered spot as far north as southern New York, where they can be planted 3 inches deep in ordinary garden soil with a winter covering of leaves. In cold areas, lift after the foliage has died and store dry until it's time to plant again. In dry summer areas, such as California, they are happy in the ground year-round. They can also be started in pots in a soilless/sand mix that drains well and then treated like freesias. Grow cool outdoors in pots until roots have formed, then bring the pots into the coolest room available and begin to water carefully until the foliage is growing well. Then continue growing in a cool, bright sunny area until flowers appear. Continue fertilizing and watering the pots until the leaves die down, then dry the pots out until it's time to restart the bulbs in fresh soil again.

Ixia conferta.

Lachenalia

(lak-e-NAY-lee-ah)

I pronounced this plant name with a hard K until I learned that it got its name more than 200 years ago from a Swiss botanist friend of Linnaeus' called La Chanel. You choose. These Cape bulbs, which look like a hyacinth with an eating disorder, are becoming more popular. They often have interesting spotted foliage, and the flowers have contrasting color combinations like green and red *(L. bulbifer)*, electric blue *(L. viridiflora)*, and orange-yellow-red *(L. aloides)*. With about a hundred species, lachenalia can take a gardener through an entire winter of flowers. Seeds are available through the Indigenous Bulb Growers Association of South Africa (see page 116) and are one of the best ways to propagate lachenalia because most species take only a couple of years from seed to flowers. As with all bulbs started from seed, I grow the plants without a distinct resting period until they go into dormancy themselves or they are old enough to place into dormancy like mature bulbs. Lachenalia will adapt to the outdoors in frostless areas in porous soil, but for me they are best planted just below the surface in pots of sandy soil mix. They like a cool greenhouse or window, and their colors develop best when the plants are grown in light shade. Lachenalia can bloom for six weeks in a cool environment. Start the bulbs in late summer for winter blooms and feed regularly. When blooming ends, reduce water until the foliage dies. Keep the bulbs dry in the pots until it's time to start the process again.

Lachenalia species. The Cape cowslip.

Lapeirousia

(lap-ay-ROO-zhah)

Lapeirousia is a genus of about 35 species from southern Africa that are sometimes lumped in with the genus *Anomatheca*, to which they are related. They are dwarf plants, only about a foot high, and grow from distinct bell-shaped corms to produce sprays of star-shaped flowers with contrasting markings in colors from blue to red. They are hardy outdoors as far north as Washington, D.C., and even farther north with protection. Plant in the garden in March for late-summer flowers or in a pot where a dozen or so corms can be planted in September for flowers by March. Water lightly at first until leaves begin to grow, then remove to a cool room and water to maintain fairly constant moist soil. After blooming continue to water and fertilize until the leaves die, and then gradually dry the soil completely until it is time to restart the bulbs. Some species of lapeirousia will bloom in a year from seed. *L. corym-*

bosa (blue flowers marked with white), *L. oreogena* (dark violet and white), and *L. silenoides* (rosy red with darker markings) are some species to try.

Lilium

Most gardeners think of lilies as hardy perennials. Many are, many others are not, and any lily can also be treated as you would other tender bulbs by planting them in pots for out-of-season flowering. The Easter lily is an example of this. I plant my lilies in pots when the bulbs arrive at garden supply stores around March in my area. I can also get lily bulbs in late summer to try over the winter. I often buy the bulk bulbs, grand old hybrids that have stood the test of time, planting four or so in a pot 12 to 14 inches in diameter in gritty loam. Use deep pots, clay or plastic, and put the bulbs well down — at least 6 inches deep. Water well and keep them in a cool room. You won't even need light until the green begins to show

Lapeirousia fabricii.

(Opposite): A group of Asiatic lilies.

Littonia modesta. Related to gloriosa, it has the typical grasping tendril tips that allow the plant to climb up to 6 feet.

on the surface. Grow them in the coolest, brightest part of your indoor growing area, putting them out only when weather permits. I get a month or two head start on garden lilies this way. When they are through blooming, I dig a hole in my garden large enough to take the whole soil ball without disturbing the roots and drop it in. They often bloom even better the next year.

Littonia

(li-TOH-nee-ah)

Littonia modesta is the best-known member of a small genus of climbing lilies from South Africa closely related to sandersonia and gloriosa. It shares some physical characteristics with these genera, particularly its grasping foliage. Littonia attach themselves to nearby plants with tendrils at the ends of their leaves. *L. modesta* has small yellow bell-shaped flowers up to 2 inches across. Pot littonia in midwinter and grow in a warm room (70°F). The secret of growing this bulb is warmth at all times, with plenty of moisture in the summer when blooms will appear. After flowering, reduce watering until the foliage dies completely, then stop watering altogether. Store the bulbs dry in the pots at 55°–60°F. These can be grown outdoors as well, but never until outdoor temperature remains warm on a regular basis.

Lycoris

(ly-KOH-ris)

I once had a correspondence with a gentleman who was puzzled and amazed that his next-door neighbor's front garden in Manitoba (one of Canada's colder winter regions) bloomed in the autumn with naked flower stems of what looked like *Amaryllis belladonna*. It turned out to be *Lycoris squamigera*, originally from Japan, one of the cooler-weather-loving members of this rewarding family. All the lycoris are from China or Japan, even the tender ones.

The tender varieties, such as *L. aurea, L. radiata,* and *L. sanguinea,* are best grown in pots with a nighttime temperature of 55°F and a cool, sunny greenhouse or window during the day. Plant in August with about a third of the bulb peeking out of a bed of rich, sandy soil in a pot just a little bigger than the bulbs. Each plant bears 5 to 20 flowers with outspread segments that recurve backward from the tips on a strong stem. The effect is charming. Flowers can be red, yellow, pink, violet, and a sort of blue. The flowers are followed by strap-shaped leaves which should be kept alive until the following summer, when they die down naturally. Follow a routine of plenty of fertilizer and water during the flowering and leafing period.

After at least a few months of total dryness, initiate the bulbs again by starting watering. If I am fortunate enough to have plenty of flowers to cut, I do so when the first buds open, and they will continue to unfold in their vase. After initial planting, avoid disturbing the roots of any member of this genus if you can. They could miss a season or two of flowering before they start to flower again.

This is a real multizone genus, well worth trying in all its forms.

Lycoris squamigera.

Moraea villosa.

Moraea

(mor-EYE-ah)

The peacock flower is South Africa's answer to the iris. Contrasting petal colors give the members of this genus its popular name, and any species offered in North America, once seen in photographs, are immediately sold out.

Some species from outside the Cape are evergreen, but this is mainly a winter-flowering corm or bulb, and once established it needs considerable moisture in a well-drained medium. Treated properly, it will bloom successively over several weeks. Moraea species are often planted near water for best results, but they cannot stand frost, so in the fall, they must be dug up. The best solution seems to be cool pot culture in deep pots to permit adequate root growth.

Seeds are about the easiest way to acquire moraea. They should be sown in a sandy medium in autumn, when the bulbs are also normally sown. Germination can take five weeks, with the medium being kept constantly moist. Fresh seed is best, and I plant it as soon as I get it from any source. Flowers arrive by the third year. In their native habitat, moraea appear at the beginning of the winter rainy period when moisture is at its greatest. After flowering, the pots should be removed to a cool, dry place for the summer dormant period.

Nerine hybrids.

Nerine

(ne-RYE-nee)

Nerine sarniensis, the Guernsey lily, has been a gardener's favorite since the 1600s, when an early shipment from South Africa, via Japan, is said to have washed ashore from a wreck on the Channel Island of Guernsey. The cargo of bulbs that washed ashore bloomed spontaneously and alerted the locals to this wonderful half-hardy bulb. Its true home wasn't discovered until the eighteenth century, when it was found growing on Table Mountain in the Cape Province of South Africa by the early Kew collector Francis Masson. It was named *Nerine* for the mythological sea nymph daughter of Nereus, and *sarniensis* is the old name for the Channel Islands.

At my house, *Nerine sarniensis*, which comes in a variety of colors from white through shades of orange and red, is grown as a pot plant. *N. bowdenii* is available in shades from pink to salmon in many named varieties that are climatically prepared to make elegant garden plants when put out in beds in the summer. Nerines will survive in the garden all year in warmer climates. For pot growth, which is how I grow all nerines, I plant the bulb when I get it. After a thorough watering I put the pot in a shaded area and wait. Flowers should appear in September to November, when I bring the pot inside for a show. Leaves that appear at this time will continue through the winter. I then fertilize well and grow my nerines in as cool and buoyant an atmosphere as possible. Leaves should be encouraged only in the winter and the spring, and then in early summer the water supply should be cut off completely until September, when the process begins again. The roots shouldn't be disturbed if possible or the plant may miss a year of blooming.

I plant the bulbs with the necks just above ground level in a sandy medium, exchanging the usual compost portion for peat moss. One noted South African authority says the original Guernsey lily grows in some of the poorest soil on earth in its native habitat. Propagate by lifting and separating the bulbs when leaves have died. This is seldom necessary in pot culture, where the bulbs grow best when they pack the pot.

Seeds germinate readily in a sandy compost, and seedlings don't take long to appear. Plant on the surface. A frost-free winter greenhouse is ideal for ripening the foliage, but a cool, bright room will do in a pinch. They are hardy in southern California.

Ornithogalum thyrsoides.

Ornithogalum

(or-ni-THO-ga-lum)

Ornithogalum thyrsoides is probably the best-known member of this genus with more than 150 species from Europe, western Asia, and Africa that range from tender to quite hardy. *O. thyrsoides* comes from the Cape and has a cone of white flowers and a strong scent. It can bloom for a month at a time, is easy to grow, and is usually available in summer bulb catalogs. You've probably enjoyed it in bouquets because florists love it for its lasting power.

I start the bulbs inside in pots as soon as I get them in late spring and transfer them outside as the weather warms up. I grow them outdoors right in the ground, by slipping them out of their pots and dropping the root ball into a prepared spot, or I leave them in their pots and water them more than those left in the ground. I take all the species indoors when frost hits. I keep them completely dry and warm, stored in paper bags in the winter.

O. saundersiae, with white flowers and dark olive green centers, is best grown as a garden specimen to bloom in late summer right in the perennial border because it can get 4 feet high at my house. I start *O. saundersiae* indoors, like *O. thyrisoides,* to get a leg up on the weather, and then transfer outdoors. After flowering the foliage begins to die down. That's the signal to stop watering altogether. If growing outdoors, I dig them up and dry them on newspapers before storing them for the winter.

Oxalis

(OX-a-lis)

Oxalis is grown by gardeners who don't even know they are growing one of the most popular bulbs in the world. Some 800 members of this genus are found all over the globe. Their leaves look like forms of giant clover and can vary from green to dark wine red, sometimes with a darker central blotch, as in *O. regnellii* 'Rosea'. The flowers of *O. versicolor* look like funnel-shaped candy canes. Most members of this genus are cheap and cheerful, which is why I like them. The tender kinds can be grown indoors. They are so vigorous, I'm always dividing portions and repotting them.

Persistent foliage is the thing with oxalis. They bloom about 6 inches high in the winter for me and then again through the summer, waxing and waning as I water more or less. Even when they are taking time off from their flowering, they look good in a window full of other bulbs. And if I want real four-leaf clover I grow

Oxalis regnellii.

Polianthes

(pol-ee-AN-theez)
This Mexican native includes about a dozen species of which the most often grown is the tuberose (*Polianthes tuberosa*), famous for its overpowering scent and virginal white color. There is also a double form called the pearl and others with a pink overlay to the blooms. Legend has it that the first polianthes bulbs arrived in Europe when a French missionary sent some to a monastery in Toulon in 1530. The monks were so fond of the flowers that it took 60 years before the first bulbs left the monastery garden.

O. deppei, from Mexico, with four red-spotted leaves with rose to reddish flowers.

The bulbs look like small pine cones and should be planted horizontally just under the surface in a 6-inch pot of humusy soil, where they will stay for years. Pot at the beginning of the growing season, which is spring for summer blooms and midsummer for fall blooms. When the flowers disappear and foliage takes a break, just slow down the watering. When new growth and flowering are not active, water just enough to keep the soil from drying out and the leaves from wilting. Propagate by planting offsets or seeds at the beginning of the growing season.

These days, tuberoses are commonly available at garden centers as summer bulbs. Look for large bulbs for best results. I plant mine in a pot in early spring in a mixture of peat and sand or soilless mix and sand, watering sparingly until the leaves appear. They can be grown in the pot, or the root ball can be taken out of the pot and planted in the garden in good soil when warm weather arrives. I prefer a pot because I've had the flowers open too late outdoors to enjoy their effect. In either case, I start the bulbs indoors by planting them in pots. Four bulbs nicely fill an 8- or 10-inch pot. I do this four to six weeks before

minimum nighttime temperatures are expected to hit 60°F. Bottom heat makes things go faster. The tuberoses should bloom in late summer. If grown outdoors, I drop the soil clump from a pot into the ground in early summer. At the end of the season, I take them out of the ground and dry them on old newspapers in a frost-free area. Tuberoses often do not bloom the second year because the clump that forms around the individual bulbs takes a couple of years to form bulbs large enough to bloom again. Anyway, tuberose bulbs are usually cheap enough so that new ones can replace the old without a major monetary outlay. Other members of this genus in-

clude *P. geminiflora,* which have more tubular, reddish orange flowers and 2-foot-long stems, and *P. howardii,* with sparser rose flowers. Try the tuberose first to get the measure of this interesting and intensely fragrant species.

Ranunculus

(rah-NUN-keu-lus)

The highly evolved and colorful *Ranunculus asiaticus* is called the Persian buttercup and has been grown in Europe and North America for centuries as a half-hardy perennial. Treat the clawlike, fleshy,

(Opposite): Rhodohypoxis
baurii growing in a spot
they like.

Romulea bulbocodium.

tuberous roots like anemone, soaking in water overnight to plump them up before planting. Place the bulbs 2 inches below the surface in the ground or a pot of rich, well-drained soil. In my area, the roots are obtained in late winter for planting in early spring. Flowers arrive by midsummer. In more frost-free locations, they are planted in late fall and allowed to grow roots over winter for earlier blooms. Keep the soil evenly moist during the growing season, drying off slightly during flowering. At the end of the growing season dry the pots completely and store the bulbs cool in the pots until the next growing season. Repot them then in fresh soil. The flowers come in multicolored mixtures of Persians, which are small; French, which are semidouble; Paeony-flowered, which are double; and Turban, which are double and look like they are on steroids, making them almost ball-like in their voluminousness.

Rhodohypoxis

(rodo-hy-POX-is)
This small genus of dwarf bulbs with huge flowers for their size is one of my favorites. There are six species, although most of us will encounter only *R. baurii* which is commonly available now in color variations of red, pink, and white flat, starlike flowers growing profusely among short, stiff, hairy leaves that make a charming combination in pots. Plant the rhizomes in the spring in a rich 50-50 mix of soil and sand about half an inch deep in shallow pans, and keep them moist during the growing season for almost continuous flowering from spring through summer. Some authorities recommend placing the pot in a pan of water to maintain continuous moisture during the growing season. During the rest period, keep the rhizomes dry in their pots surrounded by soil. Don't try these in the garden because the tiny bulbs are easily lost among other plants and can be mistaken for tiny pebbles. Rhodohypoxis can be started from seed in shallow pans of a sandy mix kept constantly moist.

Romulea

(rom-u-LAY-ah)
This large genus of star-shaped flowers with grassy leaves is found in the Mediterranean region and in Southern Africa, and because some members were first found growing near Rome, the genus was named for the legendary founder of the Italian capital, Romulus. The plants are short, usually no more than a few inches tall, with flowers ranging from white through yellow, pink, orange, rose, and magenta to a bluish purple. All have an attractive, satiny sheen to the flowers. They close their flowers in dull weather. *R. bulbocodium,* with lavender petals and yellow centers, comes from the Mediterranean

Sandersonia aurantiaca.

and is one of the easiest to try. The South African members of the genus are showier. Try *R. rosea,* with cerise pink flowers, or *R. sabulosa,* with satin red flowers with yellow and black centers that are 2½ inches across.

The tiny corms can be planted outdoors in areas that are free from frost in either spring or fall. They thrive best in a sandy, sunny spot provided with plenty of moisture during the growing season. Plant the corms about 6 inches deep. Indoors, they should be started in pots and grown or wintered in a cool green-house or bright, cool porch. Store the corms dry during dormancy, which begins when the leaves begin to wither and die.

Seed is the best way to start most of the hard-to-find romuleas, and many will bloom in a couple of years from seeds planted sparsely in pans and then divided singly into four- or six-cell plastic trays like those used to start annuals. I use this method to grow all my bulb seedlings, and it seems to work well. Grow the seedlings without a dry period until they ask for one by having their foliage dry out. At that point, keep them dry, but keep a constant eye on them and restart watering after four months if no new growth has appeared.

Sandersonia

(Sander-SON-ee-ah)

Sandersonia aurantiaca is the single member of this genus from South Africa. It is vegetatively similar to gloriosa, with which it shares a climbing, clinging habit and a similar rhizomatous rootstock. Only the orange-yellow flowers are different. They look like miniature chefs' hats or lanterns and appear from the leaf axils near the top of the 2-foot-high plants. They are best planted in wide pots in groups of four to six and look spectacular when in bloom. Although hardier than the more common gloriosa, sandersonia should also be planted in rich, well-drained soil in full sun. In autumn, I store the rhizomes dry in their pots for up to six months in a warm, dry place indoors and repot in fresh soil when the weather warms enough in the spring. In South Africa, the plant is known as Christmas bells for its flowering period, but in North America it flowers according to its planting time. That is, in midsummer if started in the spring. The rhizomes are planted horizontally a couple of inches below the soil surface and watered copiously once the upper growth starts. They will tolerate a nighttime temperature of 50° to 55°F. They are an unusual subject for growing outdoors in the summer or in a medium greenhouse or bright, cool room. The tubers are very brittle and should be kept completely dry and undisturbed in their pots for at least three or four months after the upper growth dies down. Restart by putting them in new, rich compost that contains good organic matter and plenty of grit. For best results, feed and water copiously during the active growing season so the rhi-

zomes increase in size before being put into strict dormancy. Seed-sown plants can bloom in a few years in the right environment.

Scadoxus

(Sca-DOX-us)

Scadoxus, or blood lilies, are native to tropical Africa and are still classified as haemanthus in some catalogs. The difference is that Scadoxus has rhizomes and haemanthus are true bulbs. They deserve a place in every collection. Scadoxus have starburst or bottlebrush heads of flowers at the end of a long stem and are generally grown as house- or greenhouse plants. One of the best specimens I have ever seen was growing out of a trash heap in Tobago — a starburst of red in full and rampant growth in the hot June sun, next to a rusty baby carriage. Scadoxus suf-

Haemanthus katherinae.

Sinningia speciosa. Gloxinias can be grown into huge specimen plants.

fers if grown outdoors in cooler climates. I give it as much warmth and sun as I can manage in my garden. The subspecies *katherinae* is the most likely to be found, often under the name *Haemanthus katherinae* or *Haemanthus multiflorus*, as I saw recently. These bulbs should not be dried out during the winter months, but kept only *slightly* moist during their resting period in a shady place. When they are in full growth in summer they should be watered and fertilized regularly and kept in sun or semi-shade, which is why they are such excellent greenhouse or indoor plants. They enjoy an annual top- and side-dressing of fresh soil as long as the roots are not disturbed. Don't let the bulbs dry out during storage or they will die.

Propagation is best accomplished with offsets or fresh seed sprinkled on the soil surface and left un-covered in a warm place. Some authorities recommend removing the pulpy covering on the seeds before planting to prevent rotting of the seed. In southern California, where they can be grown outdoors, seedlings will bloom the third year after sowing. Offsets can be pulled off, once they have some roots, and planted separately in pots.

Sinningia

(Si-NIN-jee-ah)

Gardeners generally call these gloxinias even though that is the true botanical name of another plant that happened to be named before this huge and popular genus. Sinningias are natives of Brazil and are usually grown as summer-blooming pot plants, although they can flower at any time, depending on when the tubers are planted. The flowers are large, velvety, and bell-shaped and come in colors ranging from white through pink, lavender, and purple, often edged and spotted with contrasting hues. The leaves, too, are velvety and handsome. A miniature form, *S. pusilla*, bears smaller violet flowers at various times of the year. Professional growers of the begonialike tubers start them from seed in a humus-rich compost in humid conditions, shaded from direct sun. They grow very well under fluorescent lights.

Start the tubers just covered with the growing mixture either in individual pots or trays with a minimum nighttime temperature of 60° to 70°F. When masses of roots have formed, transfer the tubers to individual 5- or 6-inch pots of coarse, humusy soil that has not been packed down. The soil should be kept moist but not soaking by bottom watering. Do not wet the foliage, which will spot and rot quickly. Fertilize lightly once the flower buds appear. After flowering, reduce water gradually until the foliage begins to die, then store in a warm, dry place until ready to start the process again in fresh, acid soil.

Gloxinia seed is readily available. I start mine in sandy soil sprinkled on a brick kept moist in a container of water. Once germination occurs, the tiny seedlings can be pricked out with tweezers and planted in fluffy, humusy soil and grown on. Remember that the secret to success with either growing or bringing this one back into flower from a store-bought plant is a warm and moist atmosphere.

Sparaxis

(spah-RAK-sis)

Sparaxis, or harlequin flower, comes from South Africa and includes about six species of mostly short (foot-high) plants that produce brightly colored and

Sparaxis tricolor in some of its many color varieties growing on a bulb farm.

variable flowers that account for their popular name. The commonly available rainbow mix originates from *S. tricolor.* In their native habitat, the small netted corms are planted in autumn to grow over winter and flower in the spring. They are commonly available from my local nursery at reasonable prices as summer bulbs for the rockery and make an excellent display, flowering in late summer. Plant a few inches deep in well-drained soil in full sun. In cold areas, plant sparaxis in pots in late summer and leave in a cold frame until November to form roots. Then bring in to grow in a cold greenhouse or unheated bright room for early spring blooms. Continue watering and feeding until the leaves die down in summer, then dry the pots until it is time to restart the process again in autumn.

Sprekelia

(spre-KALE-ya)

Sprekelia formosissima is the only member of this Mexican genus, and even though it was introduced to cultivation nearly four hundred years ago as the Jacobean lily, it is not as popular as it should be. Perhaps its lack of popularity is due to the fact that it produces only one flower. But what a flower. It has six velvety crimson petals that have given rise to flattering comparisons to an orchid. The long-necked black bulbs are planted one to three in a pot. In warm areas, they are grown outdoors, often under trees, where they form clumps in sun or partial shade. I grow mine in pots, burying the bulb with just the neck protruding in a rich compost-and-sand mixture. They bloom in early spring. When the

Sprekelia formosissima.
A perfect greenhouse plant, Sprekelia will also flourish outdoors in warm climates

Tecophilia cyanocrocus, the famous blue crocus of Chile, much sought after by bulb growers.

leaves begin to die I store the bulbs dry in their pots at 45° to 60°F for up to six months to make sure they bloom again the next year. When planted outdoors, sprekelias bloom in midsummer. Sprekelias are said to grow easily from seed in about three years, but I find it simpler to buy the bulbs, which are now commonly available and well worth a try for their unique red flowers.

Tecophilaea

(te-ko-fi-LYE-ah)

Tecophilaea cyanocrocus, the Chilean crocus, is probably the most famously rare tender bulb in existence. I have never owned one, so the following advice is anecdotal. Writers emphasize not only the intense blue color of the flowers, but the high cost of obtaining the tiny corms, which is the reason I've never owned one. Those who have had success with

tecophilaea plant the corms in a gritty mixture of loam, peat, and sand in autumn, placing the pots in a cold frame for a couple of months for roots to develop in the cooler conditions. As soon as the first shoots appear, put the pots in an unheated greenhouse or bright unheated sun porch for the winter, as long as the temperature does not go below freezing. The flowers will appear sometime during the winter along with the leaves. When the leaves die, keep the bulbs dormant during the summer, with an occasional moistening of the soil. Coolish conditions at all times seem to suit these bulbs best, which probably makes them most suitable for cultivation in pots in a cool greenhouse. Friends of mine who grow tecophilaea claim the corms have a disconcerting habit of not living more than a year or two, even in the hands of the best gardeners, meaning them. Of course, to a gardener this challenge makes them only more desirable. If only they were cheaper.

Tigridia

(ty-GRID-ee-ah)

Tigridia are 3- to 6-inch-diameter colorful flowers that grow from Mexico to South America. *T. pavonia* is the largest-flowered and most often grown. The flower is unusual and is shaped like a wide shallow bowl with a three-lobed edge formed by the outer segments. The three inner segments are small and flattened against the bottom of the bowl. Each flower lasts only a day, but they are impressive, and half a dozen or so will appear over the course of blooming to make it an altogether satisfying display of midsummer blossoms, particularly if grown in clumps. Some enthusiasts plant these inexpensive bulbs successively in spring to get the most display out of this unique flower outdoors in midsummer. Flowers come in white, orange, yellow, scarlet, and rose, often with a burgundy-spotted center. I treat the elongated corms like gladiolus, planting them a few inches deep in fertile, well-drained soil when the weather warms up in spring. The swordlike plicated leaves come first followed by a strong stem and upward-facing flowers that seem too large for the plant. In late autumn, I dig up the corms and dry them outdoors before storing them like gladiolus in paper bags in a frost-free place for

Tigridia pavonia. Each bloom lasts only a day, but a plant may have up to a dozen blooming in succession.

the cold months. I plant them out again by late spring. Plenty of seeds form on my plants every summer — a good way to increase a personal collection of hybrids.

Tritonia

(try-TOH-nee-ah)

There are 28 species of this South African genus that comes mainly from the Cape Province. Most of the flowers come in shades of orange to pink and white. The species *T. rosea* is said to be hardiest and can be grown outdoors in areas that do not freeze in winter. Then they really shine, spreading out like weeds. Alas, not in my yard. They do nicely as a summer bulb planted in the garden, but I have to dig them up in autumn for winter storage, dried and in paper bags. I grow *T. crocata* in pots, planting the bulbs in spring or in autumn, depending on when they were received. If planted in autumn, they should be grown through the winter and then kept dry during the summer after the foliage has been allowed to shrivel out. Early summer plantings are treated to plenty of food and water during the warm months. A dry period follows, much like that given to gladiolus. Seed germinates easily, but the bulbs are also readily available and much faster to produce a show.

Tritonia securigera. One of the first species of this genus to flower in summer.

Tulbaghia violacea, society garlic.

Tulbaghia

(tul-BAG-ee-ah)
This African genus has about 20 species of which the best-known member is *T. violacea*, commonly known as society garlic. The rhizomatous roots give rise to evergreen foliage and a 2-foot-high stalk that ends in an umbel of clear mauve flowers. A variegated form makes a nice accent plant. They make excellent ground cover in warm areas, both wet and dry, and the only serious disadvantage is the onion odor that emanates when the leaves are crushed. They are such happy growers that they are kept as houseplants by people who normally grow only the usual leafy things. Give them a cool, sunny window in winter and full sun in summer and they will thrive, bloom-

ing almost any time of year. In the North, they are best kept in pots where they can remain for years, blooming for long periods in the summer. They are somewhat frost-hardy and can be overwintered under leaves in the ground in a protected position against a sunny wall as far north as New York City.

Veltheimia

(vel-THEE-mee-ah)

The South African bulb *Veltheimia viridifolia* is for me the king of tender bulbs. Perhaps it's the dark green glossy, wavy leaves that make the plant interesting, even when it's not in bloom. The tubular pink flowers tipped with yellow are clustered on an 18-inch spike and can last up to three weeks as cut flowers. There are several color forms that range from pink to yellow. Even the seed capsules are decorative. Other species include *V. bracteata* (pink with green tips) and *V. capensis*.

The bulbs are usually planted in late autumn for a show around Christmas, and they look very rich and unusual potted in a holiday window. After flowering, the rosette of leaves will persist into spring.

Withhold water during the summer by putting the plant, pot and all, in a dry, dark, and warm place. At the end of the summer bring the pot out, top-dress it with some new soil, and water the bulb thoroughly once and then lightly thereafter until new foliage appears.

If planted outdoors in the deep South, where they can survive year-round, bury the bulbs at least a couple of inches in the soil. Pot plants should have their noses poking out of the soil. Grow in partial shade for best flowers. Seed-grown plants take about three years to bloom if grown continuously. Once mature, the bulbs should be given a definite dry period.

Veltheimia viridifolia flowers around Christmastime in pots.

Watsonia

From South Africa, these are big plants for big pots, or big spots in the garden. Some of the 52 species have flower spikes 5 feet high. They come in shades of white, pink, orange, and red through mauve. Growers in California often keep these outdoors all year, but the rest of us must treat them as tender and rely on cool greenhouses to overwinter the big plants.

Grow them like gladiolus, but give them plenty of water because their native habitat is often in moist meadow. The various species have been divided into three groups, according to their vegetation: winter growing, spring and early summer flowering (*W. meriana, W. pyramidata*); summer growing and flowering (*W. alpina, W. densiflora*); and ever-green species (*W. ardernii, W. galpinii, W. pillansii*). If climate permits, leave all groups in the ground, whether outdoors or in pots, with flowering regulated by watering according to the state of their vegetation. Keeping the plants uncrowded assures regular blooming, so divide frequently. Watsonias are easy to start from seed and should be grown continuously until they are mature enough to respond well to dry and wet cycles.

Worsleya

Worsleya rayneri is the scientific name for the spectacular empress of Brazil, the only member of this genus. The flowers resemble amaryllis but are an unusual violet-blue and are produced in summer from a huge bulb that has a neck some 18 inches

Watsonia pyramidata.

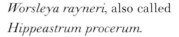

Worsleya rayneri, also called
Hippeastrum procerum.

long. Cultivation should be carried out in a tropical greenhouse in pots of acid soil that are never allowed to dry out. When planting, leave plenty of the long neck of the bulb above the soil to give the 2-foot-long sickle-shaped leaves ample growing room. A shaded greenhouse will give the right amount of light. The high humidity and moving air inside a greenhouse will duplicate the Organ Mountains, near Rio de Janeiro, where the bulbs were first discovered growing on misty cliffsides, constantly bathed in breezes. Fertilize with an acid fertilizer in spring to encourage vigorous growth. In winter, dry slightly by reducing watering, but do not dry out. Encourage new growth with more watering when warmer weather returns.

Zantedeschia

(zan-te-DES-kee-ah)
We know this as calla, or arum lily, and it is semi-hardy, surviving in many warmer areas if the tubers are buried at least half a foot underground. *Z.*

aethiopica is the classic species with white urn-shaped flowers that remind me of weddings and funerals. In their native habitat of Africa, callas flourish in wet areas and on the edge of watercourses. In cooler climates like my own, they are easily grown in pots. The rhizomes are buried in groups of a half dozen or so in large pots and watered carefully until they begin to show the spearhead green leaves with white spots that make them as attractive out of flower as in. After flowering they need a distinct rest period of at least a few months so they will flower again. A missed dormant period usually means poor, or no, flowering. Zantedeschia can be planted any time they are obtained, but late winter is the best time to start dormant rhizomes. I choose a cool, bright spot for starting them out. By the time the leaves are out it is usually warm enough so that the plants can be moved outdoors for flowering or growing if they have already flowered inside. A rich, moist soil with plenty of fertilizer in a shaded garden suits callas admirably. Clay pots can be sunk in the ground. Callas will also grow happily on the edge

Zantedeschia cultivars showing various color forms.

Zephyranthes candida. In addition to the white, there's an even more common pink form.

of a pond. By autumn they should be back indoors and drying off. Store in dry peat in a frost-free place over the winter. In the old days you could obtain only white or yellow flowers, but crosses are now available in pastels and pinks.

Zephyranthes

This native of the Americas grows from the southern United States to Argentina, with the 40 or so species ranging in color from white through yellow and pink. The single crocuslike flowers look large on the 8-inch plants when they are in flower in late spring, although the hardier *Z. candida* flowers in the autumn.

In warmer climates, up to about Washington, D.C., the bulbs can be planted 2 inches deep in autumn in regular garden soil that remains relatively dry in the winter. A covering of leaves or salt hay over winter will offer excellent protection. Where winters are frosty, plant the bulbs in spring 2 inches deep. They should be lifted after the first fall frost and stored over the winter in dry soil or peat. Pot growers can plant them more shallowly in a sandy bulb soil. If grown in a greenhouse or window, they can be planted any time as long as they get a completely dry rest of about three months after flowers and leaves have died. The bulbs increase by offsets like narcissus. Seeds germinate quickly.

Sources

VIRTUALLY ANY BULB CATALOG carries some tender bulbs, even if they are only the best-known kinds, like gladiolus and dahlia. And, of course, local sources are best for tender bulbs because then they will likely be the freshest and firmest examples of their kind. But away from large cities with established garden centers, the best way to start gathering a collection of tender bulbs is to ask at the local garden society. I have found that gardeners grow the most obscure things, and there is often someone in the neighborhood with a collection of bulbs who can help you get started.

Barring that, many of the sources listed below have some of the more unusual tender bulbs and mail-order service. Cross-border bulb buying is easier now with the Free Trade Agreement, and often no special certificates are necessary if you import bulbs from recognized sources. Your bulb seller should know if additional documentation is needed to import foreign bulbs. Usually it is hassle-free. Federal, state, and provincial agricultural inspection agencies in the United States and Canada could require Phytosanitary Certificates, Import Permits, and Freedom from Soil Certificates in certain cases, particularly when self-importing from suspect areas.

However, don't let this caution prevent you from trying out new sources. Contact your local agricultural department for further information.

Bulb seeds are free of these restrictions, and for those tender bulb growers with a nurturing bent, I highly recommend starting bulbs from seeds, particularly the hard-to-find species. You'll know the bulbs were not dug up in the wild, and by growing them from seed you will learn much about that particular bulb's life cycle.

It never ceases to amaze me that new bulbs are still being introduced regularly, even in this day and age when many gardeners are sure they've seen everything. To learn some of the practical aspects of growing tender bulbs, get the back issues of bulb journals, like that of the Indigenous Bulb Growers Association of South Africa, or *Herbertia*, the journal of the International Bulb Society, a California organization. They often have practical tips from experienced growers. This winter, when winds howl, I'll be curled up in a chair by the fireplace, a stack of plant catalogs by my side, ready to try a little tenderness.

What follows is a partial list of bulb and seed suppliers, as well as societies of bulb enthusiasts.

Bulb Sources

Kelly's Plant World
10266 E. Princeton
Sanger, CA 93657
(209) 294-7676
This company claims to have one of the biggest
canna lists around. They also carry some interesting
crinum and lycoris hybrids.

Jim Duggan Flower Nursery
1452 Santa Fe Drive
Encinitas, CA 92924
(760) 943-1658
Jim has the stock of BioQuest International, an
early supplier of unusual South African bulbs. He
also carries many irids.

Anthony J. Skittone
1415 Eucalyptus
San Francisco, CA 94132
(415) 753-3332
Large selection of South African bulbs and their
hybrids.

McClure and Zimmerman
P.O. Box 368
Friesland, WI 53935
(414) 326-4220, fax (414) 326-5769
Nice catalog with interesting information.

Louisiana Nursery
5853 Highway 182
Opelousas, LA 70570
(318) 948-3696 or (318) 942-6404
A source for tender bulbs that will grow outdoors in
the southern part of the United States.

Amaryllis, Inc.
P.O. Box 318
Baton Rouge, LA 70821
Ed Beckham
(504) 924-5560 or (504) 924-5421
The name tells most of the story, although he does
carry a number of other tropical bulbs.

Van Dyck's Flower Farms, Inc.
P.O. Box 430
Brightwaters, NY 11718-0430
Quality and price are excellent.

BRITISH, SOUTH AFRICAN, AND AUSTRALIAN SOURCES

Jacques Amand Ltd.
The Nurseries
Clamp Hill
Stansmore, Middlesex HA7 3JS
England
011-44-181-420-7110
Extensive listing.

Cape Flora Nursery
P.O. Box 10556
Linton Grange
Port Elizabeth 6015
Republic of South Africa
Good variety of both irids and amaryllids from the
Cape, including brunsvigia.

Imbali Bulbs
P.O. Box 267
Auckland Park 2006
Republic of South Africa
Robert and Andrea Orr
Extensive amaryllis and irid list.

Rust-en-Vrede
P.O. Box 753
Brackenfell 7560
Republic of South Africa
Hendrik van Zijl
Good source for bulbs and seeds of South African
species.

Sunburst Bulbs
P.O. Box 183
Howard Place 7450
Republic of South Africa
Write for list of South African bulbs.

Pine Heights Nursery
Pepper Street
Everton Hills
Queensland 4053
Australia
Carries many subtropical amaryllids.

CANADIAN SUPPLIERS

Gardenimport Inc.
P.O. Box 760
Thornhill, Ontario
L3T 4A5
Canada
(905) 731-1950
Colorful catalogs and large array of tender bulbs
and rare shrubs. Mail order.

Cruickshank's Inc.
1015 Mount Pleasant Road
Toronto, Ontario
M4P 2M1
Canada
(416) 488-8292
I bought my first tender bulbs here. Still a good
place to obtain a starter collection. Mail order.

Seed Sources

A number of the previously mentioned bulb nurseries also carry seeds, particularly those in South
Africa, so ask if you are ordering. By joining bulb societies you will receive lists of available seeds. Seeds
are a relatively inexpensive way to obtain new bulbs.
Growing bulbs from seed is surprisingly easy and
will give any gardener renewed confidence in his or
her abilities.

B & T World Seeds
Whitnell House
Fiddington
Bridgwater, Somerset
TA5 1JE
England
Ask for list number 6 (Bulbs) from their extensive
collection of many plant families.

Chiltern Seeds
Bortree Stile
Ulverston
Cumbria LA12 7PB
England
Lists many species.

Martin Kunhardt
Wahroonga
P.O. Box 144
Merrivale 3201
Republic of South Africa
Seed of brunsvigia, cyrtanthus, and watsonia, plus
hybrids.

Silverhill Seeds
18 Silverhill Crescent
Kenilworth 7700
Republic of South Africa
Rachel and Ron Saunders
Large South African bulb and seed collection.

Luis D. Arriagada G.
Casilla 8261
Vina de Mar
Chile
Rhodophiala, hippeastrum, placea, phycella species,
as well as iridacae and liliaceae from Chile.

Lachenalia liliflora

Societies Important to Bulb Growers

Nothing beats finding like-minded gardeners who will support our efforts to learn more about tender bulbs. A number of the following groups are worth joining, especially for those on the lookout for rare seeds and bulbs.

International Bulb Society
P.O. Box 92136
Pasadena, CA 91109-2136
They publish *Herbertia*, a journal for scientists and hobbyists interested in geophytes. Seed lists and seed exchange.

Indigenous Bulb Growers Association of South Africa
3 The Bend
Edgemead
Capetown 7441
Republic of South Africa
Excellent source of seeds of native South African species. Back issues of their journal provide helpful hints for new growers.

Botanical Society of South Africa
Kirstenbosch
Claremont 7735
Republic of South Africa
Growers wait impatiently for the annual seed list from the national botanic garden — one of the best sources for African plants. Publishes quarterly journal.

The Clivia Club
P.O. Box 6240
Westgate 1734
Republic of South Africa
A source of species and hybrids for one of the easiest and most popular tender bulbs.

Alpine Garden Society
Membership Secretary
AGS Center
Avon Bank
Pershore
Worcestershire WR10 3JP
England
Publishes a quarterly newsletter and seed list.

North American Rock Garden Society
Executive Secretary
P.O. Box 67
Millwood NY 10546
Publishes a quarterly newsletter and seed list.

Scottish Rock Garden Club
20 Gorse Way
Formby
Merseyside L37 1PB
Scotland
Varied seed list.

Further Reading

This is a list of some of the books I've found most useful in growing tender bulbs.

Gardening by Mail
Barbara J. Barton
Houghton Mifflin Co.
Boston
Ms. Barton's book is an excellent source for gardeners looking for any sort of plant material.

Bulbs for Summer Bloom
John Philip Baumgardt
Hawthorne Books Inc./Prentice Hall
An older source book with some excellent advice on storing bulbs, particularly in the midwestern United States.

Bulbs for the Home Gardener
Bebe Miles
Grosset & Dunlap
New York
Good hints for dealing with individual bulbs.

The Bulb Book
Paul Schauenberg
Frederick Warne and Co.
New York
Still one of the best encyclopedic reference books for all bulbs.

How to Grow Bulbs
Sunset Books
Lane Books
Menlo Park, CA
Excellent starter source for new bulb growers.

Best Bulbs for Temperate Climates
Jack Hobbs and Terry Hatch
Timber Press
Portland, OR
This book was written by Australians but is very useful for growers in North America, particularly for those who live in warmer areas.

Cape Bulbs
Richard L. Doutt
Timber Press
Portland, OR
The newest, and one of the best, sources for those interested in growing South African bulbs. Doutt grows his bulbs outdoors in southern California.

John E. Bryan: 18–19, 60, 64, 74, 83, 88, 99

Derek Fell: ii–iii, iv–v, vi–1, 12–13, 15, 55, 56 bottom, 58, 61 top, 63, 65, 71, 72, 76, 77, 85, 86, 87, 89, 91, 92, 95, 97, 98, 100, 101, 102, 103, 104, 106, 107, 108, 110, 111, 112 bottom

Charles Marden Fitch: 2, 4, 6–7, 14, 20, 24–25, 28, 32, 34, 38–39, 43, 44–45, 52–53, 54, 56 top, 57, 59 left, 61 bottom, 67, 68 top, 73, 75, 78, 79, 80, 81, 82, 84, 93, 94, 96, 109, 112 top, 116

Gardenimport, Inc.: 46, 62

Dency Kane: i, 16, 22–23, 66, 68 top, 70

Andrew Lawson: 59 right, 68 bottom, 90, 105

Alain Masson: 3, 11 top, 11 bottom, 21, 26, 33, 35, 36, 37, 40, 41, 48, 49, 50 all

Freeman Patterson/Masterfile: 17

Index

Numbers in **boldface** type refer to pages on which illustrations appear